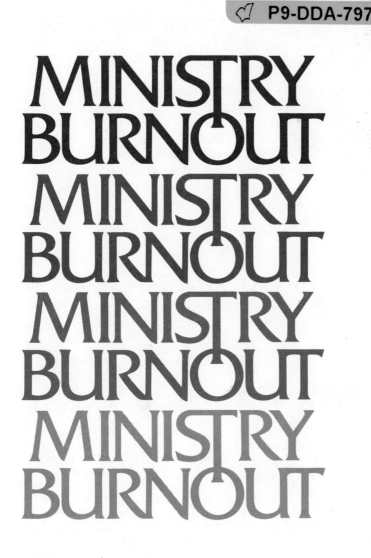

P9-DDA-797

MINISTRY
BURNOUT
MINISTRY
BURNOUT
MINISTRY
BURNOUT
MINISTRY
BURNOUT

also by John A. Sanford
published by Paulist Press

HEALING AND WHOLENESS
DREAMS AND HEALING
THE INVISIBLE PARTNERS
THE KINGDOM WITHIN
THE MAN WHO WRESTLED WITH GOD
BETWEEN PEOPLE: COMMUNICATING ONE-TO-ONE

MINISTRY BURNOUT

JOHN A. SANFORD

Paulist Press • New York/Ramsey

Excerpts from Johann Wolfgang von Goethe's *Faust*,
Part One and Part Two, translated by Charles E. Passage,
© 1965 by the Bobbs-Merrill Co. Inc.,
are reprinted with the publisher's permission.

*Unless otherwise indicated,
biblical quotations are from The Jerusalem Bible.*

Copyright © 1982 by
John A. Sanford

All rights reserved. No part of this book may be reproduced
or transmitted in any form or by any means, electronic or mechanical,
including photocopying, recording, or by any information storage and
retrieval system without permission in writing from the Publisher.

Library of Congress Catalog Card Number: 82-81190

ISBN: 0-8091-0333-8

Published by Paulist Press
545 Island Road, Ramsey, N.J. 07446

Printed and bound in the United States of America

Book design by Theresa M. Sparacio

Contents

Acknowledgments

My great thanks to Helen Macey
for her help with this manuscript,
to the clergy of the Episcopal Diocese of Los Angeles
who permitted me to speak with them
at a conference on Clergy Burnout in 1980,
and to my good friend Morton T. Kelsey,
for suggesting to me that I write this book

*Dedicated
to my father,
the late Edgar L. Sanford, II,
Episcopal Priest*

Introduction

Burnout is a word we use when a person has become exhausted with his or her profession or major life activity. Burnout has become enough of a problem to attract the attention of behavioral scientists who identify certain typical symptoms of the condition: difficulty in sleeping; somatic complaints such as weight loss, lack of interest in food, and headaches and gastro-intestinal disturbances; a chronic tiredness of the sort that is not repaired by sleep or ordinary rest and only temporarily alleviated by vacations; low-grade, persistent depression; and a nagging boredom.

There may also be uncharacteristic forms of behavior, frequently characterized by outbursts of anger or resentment. A normally patient social worker may have a sudden burst of affect at her clients; a businessman may display an uncharacteristic lack of tact with his superiors or customers; a public relations person may suddenly insult persons whose favor she should be cultivating.

Burnout can occur in many walks of life. Doctors, teachers, housewives—anyone can burn out at his or her main life activity. However this book is primarily addressed to persons whose profession it is to minister to other people through the Church. First I have in mind the clergy, but the book is also directed to others who have a ministry, such as directors of religious education, members of religious orders who function in parishes or charitable institutions, spiritual directors, and many others. While the usual context I have in mind in my remarks is that of the parish, others who have different forms of ministry in non-parochial roles should also find the discussion pertinent to their situation.

Since I am referring not only to ordained persons who are members of the clergy, but to lay persons with a religious ministry as well, I am going to use the term "ministering person" to refer to members of both groups. The term is a bit awkward, but nothing else seems to do as well. We cannot, for instance, use the word "minister" throughout since in most Protestant denominations this word refers to the ordained minister to the exclusion of the lay person. For this reason, when I occasionally use the word "minister" I mean it as the equivalent of "ministering person," and by the latter term I denote lay as well as ordained people with a professional religious vocation.

In many denominations today both men and women may become ordained priests or ministers, and in almost all denominations the ranks of the ministering persons include members of both sexes. This brings up the difficulty of what pronouns to use when a reference is made to members of the ministering professions. If "he" is used, that leaves out the women, but if "he and she" is used, that is awkward. So I am going to use "he" sometimes and "she" sometimes, both in a generic way to refer to ministering persons as a class.

The word "burnout" is not new. It is listed in Webster's New International Dictionary, which gives us three specific examples of its use: First, the word can refer to the burning out of the interior or contents of something, such as a building. Second, it can be used in the field of electricity to refer to the breakdown of a circuit owing to combustion caused by high temperatures; in this case, the conductor has been burned out by the high temperature produced by the electric current. Third, it can be used in forestry to refer to a forest fire that has been so severe that the vital humus on the forest floor has been destroyed leaving the forest denuded.

Of interest is the fact that the dictionary does not use the word with reference to human beings. To use the word "burnout" to refer to a human being's condition is a new usage of the word, and we may surmise that since the word is now used in this new way it refers to a recent social and psychological phenomenon. Not that people have not burned out at what they were doing at other times of history; that must surely have been the case. But evidently the problem is now becoming so widespread that a special word is used for the condition, a necessity that did not exist before.

It is interesting to notice how human afflictions change. At the turn of this century, for instance, the major cause of death was infectious disease, and among the most prevalent psychological afflictions was hysteria, a condition in which there is some marked physical impairment—such as the inability to lift an arm—with no physical cause. Today infectious disease as a cause of death, in industrialized nations at least, has been replaced by heart disease, arteriosclerosis, and cancer, while in the psychological realm one hardly ever encounters a case of hysteria. Instead we hear of conditions such as Burnout, and this reflects the changing conditions of human life.

If we apply the dictionary definition of burnout to

human beings, we must imagine a man or woman who has been devoured from within by fiery energy until, like a gutted house, nothing is left. Or we may imagine a person who once carried a current of psychic energy but now, like a burned out electrical conductor, cannot supply power anymore. Or an individual who, like a burned out forest, feels that her power to renew herself has been destroyed.

Our task will be to see what it is about the work of the ministering person that makes him prone to burning out, and to see if there are practical and spiritual solutions available to the person who feels he is burning out. The first part of this task will be undertaken in Chapter 1. The next nine chapters will look for possible solutions.

The final chapters will be broader in scope. The word "burnout" is drawn from the imagery of fire, and fire is a form and symbol for energy. So in its broadest scope, the problem of Burnout is a problem of energy. As both Freud and Jung have shown, each individual has a certain quantity of libido or psychic energy at her disposal, and it is this energy that enlivens consciousness and makes effective living possible. This energy can be used up, but more psychic energy can also be generated. Therefore the final chapter will look more closely at how the Ego can become exhausted when it has expended its quantity of psychic energy, and will examine some of the possible ways of renewing that psychic energy so that life can once again be effectively lived.

1

Ministry Burnout: A Special Problem

As we have already noted, many kinds of work can lead to Burnout, but the ministering person faces certain special circumstances. In this chapter I will identify nine special difficulties the ministering person faces in his work.

The job of the ministering person is never finished. People in many jobs and professions can feel that they have taken on a task and completed it. The carpenter, for instance, finishes the table he is making; the engineer can stand back and admire the bridge he has built; the surgeon may have the satisfaction of seeing his patient recover; the lawyer will eventually wind up the case with which he has been wrestling. Not so the ministering person. His work is never finished, for he faces a continuous onslaught of services, weddings, funerals, crises, parish conflicts, holy day celebrations, sick persons to see, shut-ins to visit, classes to teach, and administrative tasks. Even the dreaded Every Member Canvass seems to conclude just about in time to begin cranking up the machinery to put it in motion for the next year. Seldom can the ministering person stand back and say, "There, now that job is finished!" The ministering person is like Sisyphus in Greek mythology, whose fate it was to have to push a great stone up a mountain only to have it roll down again just before reaching the top. This feeling that a job is endless, that you never quite reach the top of the mountain no matter how hard you try, can lead to exhaustion.

The ministering person cannot always tell if his work is having any results. It can be frustrating never to have the satisfaction of seeing a work completed; it can be even more frustrating not to be sure that one's efforts are having any results at all. A house painter can stand back from his work now and then to look at what he has accomplished. But the ministering person can work for months or years and not be sure she is really accomplishing anything. This is because her work is primarily devoted to the pastoral care and spiritual nourishment of people. Are her people being helped by her ministry? On good days she may think they are, but on bad days she may be overwhelmed by a feeling that she is accomplishing nothing, and there will be nothing tangible she can point to for reassurance.

Of course there are exceptions, and one is the building program. One can stand back and admire the new building and take satisfaction in the completion of such a project (though it will not be paid for yet, of course). This may be one reason why building projects are so popular among the clergy (and among lay people too); it is a fact that money can be raised more readily for buildings than for programs. But as far as the major thrust of her work is concerned the ministering person can seldom be sure of results, and may often be preyed upon by doubts that she is accomplishing anything of lasting value.

The work of the ministering person is repetitive. Not only is the work never finished, it continually repeats itself. Christmas comes over and over, the services must be repeated, the Christmas sermon prepared, and the Christmas letter sent out to the congregation with one more attempt to present the Christmas message in an original way that will, at the same time, induce people to make extra generous Christmas offerings. The confirmation class comes over and over, and the church school program must be cranked up again each fall. One sick person recovers or dies only to be replaced immediately by another. And so it goes in what can seem like an endlessly repetitive cycle.

The ministering person is dealing constantly with people's expectations. Perhaps in no other profession, except maybe that of the politician, is a person facing so many expectations from so many people, and, to make the situation more complicated, the expectations people place upon the ministering person vary enormously. The situation can be particularly difficult for the clergy; some people expect their priest or minister to be a great teacher, others want him foremost to be a faithful pastor, others hand him the task of being a financial wizard, some want him to maintain the old traditions, but just as many may want him to be pleasingly *avant garde* (yet not threaten them too much!). Some expect him to devote himself to calling on the sick, or making parish calls, or attending community social functions, or being concerned with the poor or civil rights, while others want him for a personal counselor, or want him to be a famous preacher. On and on the list goes, and clearly no one person can be so gifted, so energetic, and so varied in his interests that he can hope to fulfill all these expectations.

Furthermore, these people with their expectations are persons who must be reckoned with. They are the ones who pay the bills. They are the ones whose favor must be won if his work is to be successful, or, sometimes, if he is even to keep his job. They can make or break the success of his program, and they can make his life agreeable or disagreeable.

For this reason, the ministering person pays a price in energy if he ignores these expectations just as he does in fulfilling them. It takes energy to contend with the rejection, criticism, or hostility of people, just as it does to please them by doing what they want us to do. Many ministering persons perform certain tasks in their work not because they want to, or even believe in their value or importance, but because it takes less energy to do the work than to struggle with people whose expectations have been disappointed.

The ministering person must work with the same people year in and year out. Taking on a parish is a little like getting married: once you get into it, you cannot get out of it easily. The doctor, lawyer, or psychotherapist may have an unpleasant client, but she also has the option of declining to accept that client, or at least the knowledge that once she has discharged her professional function she will be rid of the client. The ministering person does not have this option. She is stuck with the wearisome person in her parish and cannot avoid dealing with him; Sunday in and Sunday out he will be there to bedevil her, and maybe between times too with phone calls. The ministering person cannot afford to make an outright enemy of such an unpleasant person—he can cause too much trouble and, besides, he may have friends. So she remains in the uncomfortable "marriage" until the departure of the person or the ministering person from the parish brings relief, but of course a price has been paid for putting up with this difficult situation.

On the other side of the coin, persons whom the ministering person likes may be leaving the parish. She may spend months cultivating a relationship with certain people, may grow fond of them and rely on them, only to have them move just when her efforts seem about to bear fruit. It often seems as though the difficult people— the "parish fixtures"—never move away, but the more helpful and attractive people are always moving on. Nor is this merely a feeling, for a parish inevitably attracts a certain number of difficult personalities who cling to it year in and year out for their own reasons.

Because he works with people in need, there is a particularly great drain on the energy of the ministering person. The energy drain that comes from working with people who are in need is subtle. One hardly uses one's physical energy in working with such people, but mentally and spiritually one becomes depleted. It is like having a small but constant loss of blood. When a ministering person once complained of how tired he was getting, a colleague remarked, "Well, how many blood transfusions a day can you give to people?" That is what a person does when he ministers to someone in need: his energy is used up in supplying energy to the other person. This is so even if the person in need is a fine person whom we like; it is all the more so if the needy person is difficult, demanding, or clinging.

Of course there is satisfaction in such work when we see the person in need become better or stronger. We get energy back in the form of satisfaction when we see that the time, interest, attention, and concern we have poured out are having the desired results. But this is not always the case, for sometimes when we put energy into other people they seem unable or unwilling to use our energy investment productively. It is like pouring money down the drain. We put energy into someone, but it seems to disappear, and the troubled or difficult person remains as he was before, leaving us feeling depleted and empty.

The ministering person deals with many people who come to her or the church not for solid spiritual food but for "strokes." All of us have our genuine side and our egocentric side. The genuine part of us wants solid spiritual food so that the inner man may be nourished, but the egocentric side does not want solid spiritual food; it wants a kind of personal reassurance that will temporarily satisfy and support our egocentric attitudes and defenses. Such people do not come to church for spiritual nourishment, but to find a person or place to cling to, to be made to feel important, to hide from life and its difficulties, or to find a situation that they can dominate. These people look to the ministering person for "strokes," that is, words or actions that will meet their egocentric needs. If we give such people what they want, rather than what they need, we are somewhat in the position of St. Paul who complained that the Corinthians were infants in Christ and therefore could not eat real spiritual food. He said, "What I fed you with was milk, not solid food, for you were not ready for it" (1 Cor. 3:2).

Such people demand a lot of attention. They feel it is

their right, and if they do not receive the strokes they need and deserve they are apt to be resentful and even vindictive. Giving out strokes to such people is exhausting, but not doing so requires that a price be paid, as the ministering person now has a resentful person on her hands.

The ministering person who satisfies someone's desire for strokes may seem to benefit from receiving approval in return, but she will be what Fritz Kunkel called a "White Giant" in the eyes of others, who will elevate her because she gives them what they want. Of course she must continue to give out strokes as demanded or run the risk of suddenly becoming a "Black Giant" who refuses to make people feel better and therefore becomes the object of criticism or even hatred. We are "giants" because to many people the priest or other ministering person is elevated to a special status. But whether we are a White Giant or a Black Giant, in neither case are we being related to as we really are, for we are perceived largely in terms of whether or not we give out the required strokes.

The ministering person must function a great deal of the time on his "persona." The persona is the front or mask we assume in order to meet and relate to the outer world, especially the world of other people. The persona has a double function. One function is to help us project our personality out effectively into the world. The other function is to protect us from the outer world by enabling us to assume a certain outer posture but at the same time keep other aspects of ourselves hidden from others.

The persona is often useful and necessary. It enables us to be effective in our dealings with the world, and also to protect ourselves when that is necessary. As an example of the latter, let us say that you are a priest and are very tired, but a wedding is to take place, and even though you would rather go to the beach, you know that you must pull yourself together and perform the ceremony. To do this you put on a good front with the help of your persona—and this helps you do your job—but you keep your inward self hidden. Someone may say to you, "How are you this afternoon?" Instead of saying, "I'm worn out; I wish I weren't here," you probably will answer, "Oh, I'm just fine. Looks like this will be a beautiful wedding."

In this example the persona is helpful. Nevertheless, when we function via the persona too much of the time, and when the persona is too unrelated to the genuine personality so that other people do not see the person we really are, then we have a problem. And part of the problem is a loss of energy, for it takes a lot of energy to function through such a persona. When we are being genuine, energy flows in us naturally, but when we have to cover up part of our genuine feelings, or, worse yet, assume a posture that does not belong to us at all, a lot of energy is required.

Ideally speaking, perhaps we should always be genuine under all circumstances. It would appear that it was this way with Jesus; we have no record of his being anything other than his absolutely true self at any time. But those of us who are less well developed than Jesus must confess that at least some of the time we are forced to fall back on a persona.

The persona of the clergyman may be partly a posture he adopts for himself, and partly a mask that others hand him to wear. Many a clergyman decides, "As a minister I am going to be a good guy, always nice, loving, and pleasant." He is then stuck with that, and has to assume that posture even if he should be angry, feel in an ugly mood, or be concerned with his own needs to the exclusion of the needs of others. But it also happens that a congregation hands the ministering person a persona, and when he fails to live up to it there is a definite reaction on the part of many people.

Part of this collective, professional persona is that the ministering person is not to be angry. Yet, like anyone else, we can get angry, and sometimes our anger is not only justified but healthy. One clergyman told of a class he was teaching that was repeatedly interrupted by a young man who asked annoying and irrelevant questions in such a way as to disrupt and impede the class. This young man was a stranger to the clergyman and he tried to deal with him tactfully and kindly, but as he became more irritating the clergyman became angry and finally decided to express his anger openly. That settled matters with the young man, who caused no more difficulty, but afterward the clergyman received several letters from people who had attended the class expressing shock that he had become angry. Interestingly enough, the young man phoned the clergyman the day after the class, asked for an appointment, told him that he realized he needed help, and asked where he could go to find it.

The problem of the public persona of the ministering person has been around for a long time in the Church. We find it, for instance, in the First Epistle to Timothy, where we are told:

> To want to be a presiding elder (priest or bishop) is to want to do a noble work. That is why the president must have an impeccable character. He must not have been married more than once, and he must be

temperate, discreet and courteous, hospitable and a good teacher; not a heavy drinker, nor hot-tempered, but kind and peaceable. He must not be a lover of money. He must be a man who manages his own family well and brings his children up to obey him and be well-behaved: how can any man who does not understand how to manage his own family have responsibility for the church of God? He should not be a new convert, in case pride might turn his head and then he might be condemned as the devil was condemned. It is also necessary that people outside the Church should speak well of him, so that he never gets a bad reputation and falls into the devil's trap (1 Tim. 3:1–7).

And elsewhere we read:

You must aim to be saintly and religious, filled with faith and love, patient and gentle.

Now no one can be saintly and religious, filled with faith, love, patience and selflessness all the time. We can strike a pose and seem to be this way, but if it is not what we genuinely are and feel at the time, we are not real but something of a fake. As I have shown in Chapter Six of my book *Evil: The Shadow Side of Reality*, we will lose touch with our genuine self if we try to be something we are not. To assume a persona such as the one described in 1 Timothy will not only exhaust us, because it takes energy to pretend to be something we are not, but will also impoverish our personality, and, in the long run, also impoverish our congregation. Yet if we depart from such a persona—by displaying anger, for instance—many people will be shocked, and we may have to pay the price of their disapproval.

The ministering person may become exhausted by failure. This is perhaps the most important source of Burnout. In the fall of 1980 I was asked to talk on the subject of Clergy Burnout at a clergy conference. I had discussed many of the reasons for Burnout that I have just reviewed when one of the clergy came up and, practically with tears in his eyes, said, "You have forgotten the most important reason of all—failure."

What constitutes failure in the ministry? When we look more closely at this reason for Burnout we will try to answer this question. For now suffice it to say that if, for whatever reason, a ministering person feels that he has failed, this will become a major source of Burnout.

All of this is the dark side of the life of the ministering person. There is also the positive side: the fine people with whom the ministering person works, the support one gets, the satisfaction of helping people, the spiritual help from the Eucharist, the worship and the life of the Church, the variety of work to do in a parish, and many other benefits.

It is important to recognize this positive side of the ministering person's life and work, but the happy things in life do not require books to be written about them, so in this book we must deal largely with the unhappy side. The fact is, that in spite of the positive side of his work, the ministering person can get burned out if enough of the above-mentioned negative factors also exist. Because of these negative factors, the fire of energy may go through the ministering person to his work and people, and leave him empty. So without overlooking the positive side, we will go on to look more deeply at these negative and defeating factors, and see if we can find ways to resolve, or at least help, with the problems.

In the following chapters I will take up each problem in turn. Three approaches to the problems will be undertaken: First, certain practical suggestions will be made when possible. Second, the problem will be looked at in the broader scope of the spiritual life. Third, the psychology of the ministering person will be examined to see if there are ways that the individual can mitigate the problem by dealing more realistically with himself. For it is a fact that ministering persons are seldom just the innocent victims of negative factors beyond their control; they are also secret contributors to their problems because of their own hidden egocentric attitudes. When we are victims, it is sometimes because we have the psychology of victims, so an effort will be made to ferret out possible underlying psychological reasons that may predispose us to burning out at the difficulties that we face in our work.

2

The Problem
of the Endless Task

"The job of the ministering person is never finished."

As we have seen, the work of the ministering person is never completed. As the years roll by, this can deplete energy to the point where the ministering person becomes burned out.

When faced with such endless work the crucial factor may be whether or not we can cultivate the correct, saving attitude toward it. My father was an Episcopal clergyman, and when he was a young man and I was a boy I remember that he worked what seemed like endless hours. All day, most evenings, and often seven days a week he would labor at his parish duties. He was effective too: a respected priest, efficient rector, and a good pastor. But later in his life he changed. He still worked hard and effectively (perhaps more effectively than before), but he did not work endlessly. I remember that once he said to me, "I used to work all the time. Now I decide what is an honest day's work and do it and then go home."

The fact is that the ministering person is the only

person who can resolve many of his problems. This was my father's way of dealing with his problem of the endless work a pastor has to do. Of course, if there was a crisis in the parish he would respond to it, but the fact is that there are few crises that cannot be resolved during the ordinary work day or cannot wait until tomorrow. My father's practical attitude toward his work day made life better for him—and his family—and enabled him to keep working as a priest all of his life.

There is also the professional writer who once said, "I never finish a manuscript; I finally just abandon it." Manuscripts are like parishes; the work is never done. No matter how many times you go over a manuscript you can see new changes that need to be made, sentences that could be written a little better. But eventually we must decide that what we have done is good enough, and let the manuscript stand as it is. So it is many times with the work of the ministering person.

My father-in-law, who is a doctor, once heard me complaining about my work. I can still remember what he said to me, not in a chastising way, but reflectively, as though he were thinking back to his own problems with his work as a young man: "Every man must learn to live with his profession."

A ministering person enters his profession, not for just a few years, but with the expectation of serving for a lifetime. For this reason he must find a way to work at a pace that can be maintained for a long period of time. He must learn to think like a long-distance runner, who knows he has a long way to run and cannot afford to exhaust himself by running the first part of the race faster than a pace he can maintain.

Sometimes the ministering person becomes inflated with a sense of his own importance and concludes that if he does not work endlessly the world will come to an end. But not even God worked endlessly, according to the Book of Genesis, for the Creator, after working for six days to create the world, rested on the seventh day. The ancient Hebrews wisely decided to follow the divine example and carefully observed the commandment, "Thou shalt keep holy the sabbath day."

The ministering person cannot always keep the seventh day holy as a day of rest, since Saturdays and Sundays involve many parish duties, but he can take another day each week as a day of rest. Keeping this day holy means reserving it for oneself and one's own soul. Obligations to the parish, our usual duties, and serving the needs of others (except one's family) are to be postponed until the next day.

It is important that the day off (or two days off) be kept sacred, with none of the usual activities, because the purpose of such a day is to enter into a new state of consciousness. By removing yourself from your usual surroundings and tasks you allow a new consciousness to take shape. But it is like going swimming—you need to get all the way into the water. If the day is broken up by some official task, the new kind of consciousness that is beginning to develop is broken. That is why just a few hours off here and there do not renew us sufficiently. It takes longer than that for the invisible threads that connect us to our work to be relaxed so that new thoughts, new moods, new experiences, can find their way in.

Ministering people are notoriously poor about keeping even one day of the week sacred for themselves and their families. They always have a score of reasons why it cannot be done. This or that simply *must* be done; there is a crisis that cannot be postponed; the secretary must have some work finished by us at a certain time; some church group which is meeting that day would not understand it if we were not with them. It is remarkable how many things suddenly become much more important than our own souls and our own renewal, in spite of the commandment to keep holy the sabbath. Then, often with a martyred or "noble" or long-suffering look on our face we show up for work as usual.

We act as though we cannot help working so many days a week, but often the truth is that we prefer to work. If we are not working, we may have to spend time with ourselves, and this can be surprisingly difficult, for we may not find our own company very enjoyable (though why we should foist ourselves off on other people when we cannot bear to be with ourselves is hard to understand). We may also lose our sense of value when we are not working. Only when we are working very, very hard do we feel affirmed that what we are doing is important. As soon as we stop, doubts begin to come in, and vague feelings that perhaps what we are doing with our lives and ministries isn't so essential after all. To keep away these plaguing doubts we plunge into work, hard work, constant work, reassuring ourselves in this way that we must be important people doing important things.

We may also work seven days a week to avoid our home life. If we stay home, there may be the difficult matter of being with the children, or having to relate to our wife (or husband) who, since she (or he) almost certainly feels neglected, may prove to be a problem. But if there is the hospital call we *have* to make, then with a "good conscience" we can avoid the unpleasant confrontation. After all, it is God's work we are doing isn't it? Ministering people, and doctors too, are good at this. They can escape from entangling family difficulties any time they like, for there is always some sick person to be seen, some crucial matter to be taken care of. And, we think to ourselves and tell our families, is this not God's work which supersedes all other responsibilities?

In short, if our work is swallowing us it may be because we want to be swallowed. To solve this problem we must look into ourselves to discover what inadequacies or what personal needs in us we are trying to cover up by our immersion in work. We may have to look at some unpleasant facts in this process, but we can be sure of this: the price will be paid somewhere. If we do not pay the price creatively by examining ourselves creatively and carefully, we will have to pay the price later in the form of exhaustion with our work, broken relationships, or a life that has been incorrectly lived.

3

The Airy Work
of the Ministering Person

"The ministering person cannot always tell if his work is having any results."

As we have seen, because the work of the ministering person concerns people and spiritual matters it is often hard for him to see concrete results from his labors. Spiritual work has an airy quality about it. It is real, but intangible to the physical senses, and therefore it is hard to see the results of our efforts. As we have noted, while some people can stand back and actually see what they have accomplished, the ministering person can work and work and never be sure that anything is happening as a consequence.

We cannot change the nature of our spiritual work, but we can sometimes help ourselves by finding some work on the side that compensates the airy nature of our spiritual work. This other work needs to be involved with something tangible and solid in order for it to be renewing. In order to discover what this work might be we need to find the other kind of man or woman in us. We are not just a minister; there is another person in us who could do other things.

We can think of this other person as the physical one who works with hands and body. He or she may be a carpenter, metal worker, sculptor, farmer, woodsman, cook, artist, or athlete. This person will be the one who works with solid, tangible reality, and produces definite results: the finished table he has made, the gourmet dinner she has prepared, the garden he has created, the lovely picture she has painted, or whatever it may be.

To work with the psyche, the spirit, the world of words and people and their problems, is to run the risk of becoming psychologically thin. To find the other person in us who works with the realm of the tangible is to become solid again; it has the effect of coagulating our personality, as it were.

A story I told in my book *Healing and Wholeness* is worth repeating at this point. A musician was in a terrible depression and no amount of psychology or prayer seemed to help. He was driving home one day when he had a flat tire. He got out of the car and inspected the depressing situation, went to the trunk and fumbled around for the jack. He could not remember when he had last changed a tire and had all but forgotten how to use the tools. He worked for over an hour changing the tire, and when he had finished he was completely out of his depression. He could not understand it, but he felt like a new man.

Later he had a dream of a large, strong black man with tools in his hands. Taking the cue from the dream he purchased some tools, followed some impulses in himself he had submerged, and proceeded to remodel part of his house. His music became meaningful again; the work with the tools brought him renewing energy that revitalized, rather than detracted from, his main occupation.

My father also had the tool-using man in himself and instinctively developed it. He was never happier than when he was in a hardware store. He had his tools in the old barn at our summer home in New Hampshire all carefully arranged. Each one had its proper place, hung on its special hook, or kept in its special drawer, meticulously and lovingly cared for. And of course he used them constantly during his month's vacation when he forgot that he was a minister for a while and lived the life of a farmer, carpenter, and metal worker.

Christianity is the religion of the Incarnation. It says that God became man, that the Word became flesh. This means that the world of concrete reality, of the earth and the body, is as holy as the world of the spirit and the mind. In fact, our spiritual side is increased and enhanced by the development of the physical man, just as our physical side is enlivened by our spiritual life. We are truly a whole organism, and if any part of us—body or spirit—languishes, the whole is affected.

Jesus himself would seem to have been a man with earthy qualities, and this is reflected directly in his sayings. One way to know which of the sayings ascribed to Jesus in the Synoptic Gospels are authentic and which are accretions from the early Church is the test of earthiness. The earthy sayings bear the mark of originality; those sayings that lack this quality are open to doubt. When Jesus is quoted as having said, "No man, having put his hand to the plow, and looking back, is fit for the kingdom of God," we may be fairly sure that we are reading what Jesus actually did say. Similarly when he says, "Consider the lilies, how they grow; they toil not, they spin not; and yet I say unto you, that Solomon in all his glory was not arrayed like one of these," we may again be sure that this is an authentic saying of Jesus. For, unfortunately, we do not find this earthy quality in the teachings of the early Church.

Perhaps one reason why more of us do not develop the physical man is because we tend to be spiritually lazy. As long as we are performing our priestly and parochial tasks the way is laid out for us. Then we *know* what to do, and all we have to do is follow the well-laid-out road. Even though we may grumble and complain, what we are supposed to be doing is clear. But if we discover the other man or woman in us and find out what a physically oriented life would be like, we have to go an individual way. No one can tell us who this other person is but ourselves. We have to discover this other person by following the clues given us by our fantasies and impulses, and we have to find an original way of expressing this other side of us that fits our individual personality and circumstances. To function as the ministering person we have outer sanctions telling us what to do and how to go about it. To develop the other one in us we have to be motivated and guided from within. Out of sheer spiritual laziness many of us neglect this inner one and the cultivation of the physically oriented side of life, because we are, without realizing it, unwilling to depart from the conventional path. If this is the case, then of course we need to look to ourselves and see how we are contributing to our own problems.

4

The Revolving Wheel

"The work of the ministering person is repetitive."
We have seen how the work of the ministering person repeats itself. Our work can make us feel like Ixion, the figure of Greek mythology who was bound to a wheel that revolved endlessly through the heavens. This is a special problem, for repetitive work loses its creativity. The first number of times we perform a certain function it may bring us energy, but eventually we wear out the creativity of the work because we have repeated it so often. Exhaustion and boredom are the inevitable result.

Teachers know this. If they teach the same course and the same material year in and year out it becomes tiresome. Pastors, who are also teachers by the nature of their work, are equally susceptible to this difficulty.

Though the ministering person cannot entirely avoid the repetitiveness of her work, there is also a certain amount of autonomy in her work. To a large extent the ministering person has the privilege of choosing where to spend her time and energy; this is one of the positive aspects of religious work. It helps offset the wearing effects of repetition to have some aspect of the work that is fresh and new. This work should involve us in our growing edge, giving expression to our latest ideas or interests, and thus putting us in touch again with creative energy.

A class in which we can teach what is most interesting and new to us, a group with which we can share our deepest concerns, a new way of reaching out to people with which we can experiment—all of these may involve our growing edge and be an antidote to the problem of repetition.

It also helps, of course, to get away from our work; in fact, if the example of Jesus shows the way, it is necessary. We read repeatedly in the Gospels that Jesus, after a period of active ministry, would retire into the wilderness to be alone. Luke tells us, "His reputation continued to grow, and large crowds would gather to hear him and to have their sickness cured, but he would always go off to some place where he could be alone and pray" (Lk. 5:15–16). We are talking now, not of a simple day off, but of an extended period of time in which one withdraws from the revolving wheel of repetitive work and seeks the special renewal that can come from a total change of activity, people, and geography.

After working for twenty-three years in one parish, my father finally resigned. He confessed to me, "I've done everything I can think of to do." There were no more fresh, creative possibilities for him in his work, and so he left, even though at the time he had nowhere else to go. Eventually he was called to a new parish, but this time he was careful to make an agreement with his Vestry: he would work four days a week, but it was understood that three days during the middle of the week he was free to go to his New Hampshire farm. Of course my father had reached the point in life where such privileges can be requested, and the work to which he went was, deliberately, not as demanding as the work from which he had resigned. Still, he recognized the importance of "going to the wilderness" at regular, periodic times in order to avoid the danger of exhaustion through the revolving wheel of parish life.

The fact is, it is not always so easy for people to benefit from their time away from their regular routine because they often do not know how to use that time as beneficially as my father did at that point in his life. Going on a vacation may not be the answer because the vacation may turn out to be an empty, fruitless, or even spiritually dangerous time. The word "vacation" and the word "vacate" both come from the Latin word *vacare* which means "to be empty." For some people a vacation may be simply that: a time of emptiness. They have vacated their usual responsibilities, but have moved into emptiness, not into fullness.

It is well known that when we are empty we are open to bad experiences. Jesus warned us of this in the parable of the man whose unclean spirit left him, but when it returned and found the home empty and tidied, it went out and collected seven other spirits worse than the first (Mt. 12:43). The empty soul and the empty life are susceptible to evil. This is why many people find that their vacations are not refreshing experiences, but lead to quarrels in the family, depression, or boredom, and they are relieved to get back to the comforting monotony of their regular lives.

For this reason it is often better to plan a pilgrimage instead of a vacation. A pilgrimage also is time away from the regular routine, but it involves a journey or sojourn for a planned and sacred purpose. When people go on pilgrimages they leave their usual lives and journey somewhere for a definite reason that has to do with their development; they are pursuing something they wish to learn, or an experience they hunger to have.

Time spent at an interesting conference, a trip to see some special country or people, getting away in order to undertake some particular study, going to a certain place because there is something there that is inherently interesting—all of these may represent taking a pilgrimage. Often it is the best "vacation" that we can take, and a way to interrupt the revolving wheel.

The resolution of the problem of repetitive work requires originality on our part. Only a creative solution will help, and, as the following story tells us, an egocentric attempt at a solution may make the problem worse.

In her book, *The Feminine in Fairy Tales*, Marie-Louise von Franz discusses the fairy tale "The Handless Maiden." The story begins with a miller whose once-flourishing business has begun to decline. While contemplating his depressed state of affairs the miller encounters the devil, and the devil offers to revive his business for him and see to it that it prospers if the miller will give him the first thing he sees in his back yard when he returns home. The miller remembers the old apple tree in his back yard, and thinks to himself that he would never miss that, and so he agrees to the bargain. Unfortunately, when he returns home and looks into his back yard the first thing he sees is his lovely daughter. The miller is terribly shocked and distressed, but a bargain is a bargain (besides, he wants his mill to prosper again!) so he gives his daughter into the devil's power, the devil fulfills his part of the bargain, and the mill prospers once more.

The fairy tale goes on to the adventures of the miller's daughter, but what concerns us here is the miller. As von Franz points out, the miller was one of the first mechanics, and his work prospers because in the mill a wheel goes round and round repeating work in a mechanical way. The fairy tale thus depicts exactly the state of affairs we are considering: a situation in which a person has done work of a revolving sort that once flourished but, because it has become mechanical, is now depressing. The story tells us what *not* to do to solve the problem, i.e., don't sell our souls to the devil. Yet that is exactly what many people do. Rather than find a creative solution to their difficulty, they make a renewed effort to keep the old machinery going at any cost, and though they may continue for a while to have outward success, they lose their souls in the process.

With both men and women, repetitive work, done mechanically and lacking in creativity, affects the feminine part of them negatively. Like the miller's daughter, it goes to the devil, and with the loss of this feminine side our life loses its color, our minds lose their imagination, and our emotional life atrophies. The price we are now paying for the continued success of our work has become too great. As Jesus reminded us, "For what is a man profited, if he shall gain the whole world, and lose his own soul?" (Mt. 16:26 KJV).

If, like the miller, we have tried to solve the problem of declining enthusiasm for our work by a devilish scheme to keep it going at all costs, of course we need to examine ourselves. Where has our creativity gone that we cannot come up with a better answer? Why are we not capable of a more original response? How did it happen that our egocentric concern with our worldly success took us over to such an extent that we would sacrifice our most precious values? Once again the problem of the ministering person may lie, not just in the nature of his work, but in himself. Are we such a "Star" that life is only bearable when we are the center of admiration? Are we driven by our own desperate insecurity to maintain our power position at all costs? If so, instead of finding a creative solution to our problem that comes from our inner Center, we may be driven to desperate efforts to keep the show going so that our shaky sense of our own value remains intact. Obviously such a solution to our problem is not for the glory of God, but for the glory of our Ego, although, being very clever, we can disguise this fact from ourselves, and perhaps from other people as well.

5

Dealing With Expectations

"The ministering person is dealing constantly with people's expectations."

As we have seen, the ministering person is faced with so many different expectations that they can never be satisfied. He can wear himself out trying to satisfy these expectations, or exhaust himself in anxiety because he cannot.

Sometimes there are practical measures the ministering person can take to ease his problem. One is to clarify the expectations placed upon him by his Vestry, Board, Parish Council, or other official body to which he is responsible. It may be that the people most concerned with the minister's performance, and the minister himself, may agree on his most important tasks. Even if they do not agree, the matter needs to be brought into the open so that people will understand each other, thus easing the tension. It almost always helps to have a difficulty openly discussed rather than to let it smolder inwardly.

Of course there will be other people with expectations who are not on the official boards or committees we work with, but it will still help to work matters out with the people to whom we are most responsible.

One clergyman promised his Board that in the summer he would undertake a house-to-house neighborhood calling campaign in order to satisfy his Board's ambitions for an increase in the membership of the parish. But as the time drew near he felt deeply burdened with the thought of this work. Not only did he lack the kind of energy such calling took, he also doubted its efficacy. Yet he felt that he was expected to do it (which he was). Finally he took his problem to the Board and shared it with them frankly. The result was that the lay people changed their expectations, and it was agreed that such calling would not be a good expenditure of their pastor's time and energy. In this way the matter was resolved to everyone's satisfaction.

Another solution is to refuse to accept certain tasks that people want us to undertake. This way we can avoid some expectations because we make it clear from the start that we are not going to fulfill them. For instance, a parishioner may ask a clergyperson to call upon someone who has a particular problem: the So-and-so's are having marriage problems, or a certain person is drinking too much, or another person is lonely. Perhaps the clergyperson cannot, or is unwilling to make such a call because he is overloaded already with calling responsibilities, or because he feels that he can only be of help to people when they, on their own initiative, ask for his help. Yet most ministering people will agree to make the call and then go through the agony of *not* making it, carrying around with them the burden of an unfulfilled expectation.

It helps to remember that in such a situation we

have the option of being perfectly frank and saying at once that we are unwilling to accept the responsibility of making the requested call. The reason we give can be equally frank: "I don't have the time . . . I do not believe in such calls . . . I cannot accept any more responsibility."

Naturally, when we declare that we will not make the requested call it will sound like a kind of atrocity. A clergyperson not willing to make a mercy call! But it is better right away to make a clean admission that we are not going to fulfill the request than it is to have someone disappointed with us because we do not do it. It is also surprising how accepting people are of such frankness.

By the way, this also gives us the choice of making the call later anyway. I am reminded of Jesus' parable of the man who had two sons. He went to the first son and asked him if he would work in the vineyard that day, and this son answered, "I will not go." But afterward he changed his mind and went. The man said the same thing to the second son, who said that he would go, but in fact he did not (Mt. 21:28–31). As Jesus reminds us, it is always better to be in the position of the first son than in that of the second.

The advice that Machiavelli gave to would-be tyrants in his book *The Prince* is timely here. This is hardly the sort of book we would ordinarily look to for spiritual advice, but in this case Machiavelli's advice bears out Jesus' cryptic saying, "For the children of this world are in their generation wiser than the children of light" (Lk. 16:8, KJV). What Machiavelli said was that if in order to achieve power you have to commit atrocities, it is better to commit them all at once and in the very beginning. Whatever you do, he warned, do not string your atrocities out. If refusing to agree to call upon someone seems to you like an atrocity, it may be better to commit it in the beginning by saying no to the request.

In meeting the expectations of people it also helps to have a balanced church staff. This is only possible, of course, if the church is large enough to support a multiple-ministry. People differ in typology and interests, so try to gather a staff with varied psychological attributes and interests. If the pastor is a good preacher and teacher and likes the world of ideas, there should be an assistant who likes pastoral work and making calls, or a religious education director who enjoys an aspect of the work that the pastor does not. In this way different people will be working to satisfy different expectations from the congregation.

If we happen to be the pastor in charge, we need to get the best people we can to assist us. Sometimes the ministering person in charge is so in need of adulation from his people that he only brings inferior people onto the staff so that his glory will not be diminished. Or he finds a way to keep his assistants from fulfilling their ministries or getting their share of credit for their work because his Ego is so insecure that he is threatened by the success of anyone else. Actually it works the other way around: effective people on the staff will enhance rather than detract from the reputation of the pastor. Some of the credit that his assistants receive for their good work will also go to him for being wise enough to have such good people on his staff.

We want to be aware that some of the expectations we worry about may not be coming from others but from ourselves. It is as though there is a "Voice of Expectation" within us, an "Inner Monitor" or "Inner Secretary" who continuously admonishes us about what we should be doing and keeps careful track of all our failures and omissions. This inner voice makes itself felt in a series of autonomous thoughts that arouse guilt and anxiety.

The Inner Monitor easily gets projected onto outer people, which means that we suppose other people are expecting certain things from us when in fact the expectations come from within ourselves.

I recall a ministering person on the staff of a large church who received a message to return a phone call from Mr. X. Now Mr. X was a "big man" in the church, one of its pillars, and he was, in this person's eyes, an awesome and critical father. All day he sweated out the phone call he had to make. His imagination went wild, and his Inner Monitor told him that Mr. X had called to tell him how he had failed in this or that. When he finally made the call, Mr. X told him, "I just called to tell you what a great job I thought you did last Sunday." This is projection; the negative thoughts were not in Mr. X, but in the ministering person's own mind.

The Inner Monitor seems to speak with the voice of God. That is, we hear this voice with its "shoulds" and "oughts" speak with great authority. But though it poses as God, upon closer examination we will find that it is built up from the collective expectations of many people compounded with our own fear of failure and guilt.

The voice of the Inner Monitor tends to operate from the background. We may hardly be aware of it, yet it fills our minds with these guilts, fears of failure, and concerns about unfulfilled duties. It helps if we can bring this voice out into the open and face it. This is done by taking these thoughts that have been speaking from the wings of the stage, as it were, and forcing them to come out to center stage where they can be examined. Then we can have it out with them and decide for ourselves what we are to do with our ministries.

We can even carry on a dialogue with this voice; we can listen to these thoughts and then answer them. If we write down the conversation that follows it has more reality for us, and more healing power. It is not hard to carry on this dialogue once we spot the thoughts of the Inner Monitor. After all, this inner voice is speaking to us all the time; all we need to do is record the thoughts and answer them, and a dialogue is under way. Such a process tends to lessen the tyrannical power of the inner voice, strengthen the Ego, and make it more likely that we will find a creative solution to our difficulties.

One reason that the Inner Monitor has such power over the ministering person is because of the amount of guilt most religious professionals carry. As we have seen, the religious professional can be burdened with the feeling that he *has* to be good. As ministers we feel that we are supposed to be loving and unselfish, always kind and concerned with the welfare of other people. We are not allowed by our Inner Monitor to have a Shadow, that is, a dark side with its own impulses, needs, and desires. We may make a great effort to fulfill this goodness, but the result will be weariness of soul and exhaustion. Being unnatural and inspired by guilt instead of genuine love, it will not be goodness but a subtle form of egocentric posturing. We will have forgotten the Gospel with its message of salvation through grace, and will have relapsed into the idea of salvation by good works.

Frankness and genuineness are always more healing than the best of egocentric posturing, as in this example. A young woman consulted a pastor for counseling. After the interview she wrote to him that she would not come back because he did not seem to care enough for her. "I came to you," she wrote, "to find the love of Christ, but you did not seem to be that concerned about me."

In his reply the pastor said that it was no doubt true that he did not love her as she wanted, but if she wanted to find the love of Christ, she must find Christ. He was not Christ, but only human; his love was imperfect and he could not promise to show her Christ's love. But, he added, if she wanted to come back and talk again he could assure her that he was interested in her and would try to help her. She did come back, and the counseling work that followed proved fruitful; the pastor's honesty made this possible.

The ministering person's proneness to guilt makes her vulnerable to manipulation. Clever people, including con artists, sense this weakness in the clergyperson and can use it to make her their victim. They can even extract money from her if they can prey on her fear of being guilty. As soon as a ministering person learns to deal with her guilt, all of this manipulation comes to an end.

It is also guilt that makes it difficult for a ministering person to work effectively with potential suicides. Such people often do this because it will get them a lot of attention and not because they are serious about it. It enables them to control the ministering person, and they may intrude on her private life, call at all hours of the night and disturb her sleep, or make undue demands upon her working time.

These cases can be exhausting, and the mental stress and loss of sleep over a prolonged period of time can be a threat to health. For some reason people assume that they have the right to intrude upon a ministering person even if they are not members of her congregation. It can get so she hates to hear the phone ring for fear of who may be calling with a demand that she will feel she must fulfill.

One clergyman related how he finally got to the end of his rope with such calls. He always felt impelled to see the person, and his Inner Monitor told him that it was his divinely ordained duty to respond to such calls. What if he did not and the person *did* commit suicide? That seemed like an awesome guilt that he could not face. But eventually he was driven to his limit. He felt that his own health was threatened, and he finally became angry with an anger born from a healthy urge for self-preservation. Wisely he directed his anger at God, to whom he said, "From here on, Lord, *You* are responsible for these people. Do not put them on my back. You created them, and whether or not they commit suicide is between them and You. If You do not want them to commit suicide, then do something about it. I am resigning from the role, and will not carry that responsibility any longer."

Somewhat to his surprise, lightning did not fall upon him from heaven. To the contrary, he at once felt much better. And he also found, somewhat to his surprise, that no one committed suicide because of his new stand. He even found that he could tell people frankly that if they decided to commit suicide, that was their choice, but they had better think twice about it because God might not like it if they gave up the fight before the game had ended. In fact, he was more helpful with these people after he had disclaimed responsibility than he was before, and certainly he was a healthier person and his ministry became more enjoyable.

Once again we see that the resolution of the problems of the ministering person may require resolving certain problems within himself, as well as practical solutions involving changes in his outer life. The more growth there is in the ministering person, the more likely it is that he will be able to cope with the difficulties of the ministry without becoming exhausted, and, of course, the more helpful he will be to his parishioners.

6

Help Through Relationship

"The ministering person must work with the same people year in and year out."

Imagine you are going on an ocean voyage. The passengers all tramp onto the ship, and you are one of them. When everything is ready the boat sails. As time goes on you will get to know some of the other people on the ship. Some you may like, and some you may not like, but there is no getting away from them until the boat reaches its destination. For the duration of the voyage you are going to be together, like it or not.

The situation is much the same with a ministering person who works in a parish: like them or not, the members of the parish are people from whom the minister cannot get away. Fortunately, most people in the parish will probably be fine people whom the minister will like, but there are bound to be a few people who prove to be difficult.

Here is a problem that cannot be avoided, but we can find help by developing other relationships, not in terms of our profession, but in a personal way. We need relationships in which we can just be ourselves, where others will relate to us just as human beings, and the professional aspect is not part of the relationship.

Among members of the parish this is not always possible because almost everyone in the parish will relate to the ministering person in terms of his profession. Let us go back to our analogy of the sea voyage, but imagine this time that you are the captain of the ship instead of a passenger. All the other people on the ship will relate to you in your capacity as captain. Some will be other officers or crewmen who will see you as the authority; the passengers will see you as their benefactor, or the one who is to perform a service for them. It will be a rare thing if there is someone on board who relates to you just in a human way without regard for your position as captain. It is much the same with the ministering person in a parish situation.

One priest found that it became important to him to wear his clerical collar less and less. He still wore the clerical clothing when performing the sacraments, or when acting in his official, priestly capacity, but on many other occasions he went without it. He was startled to find that when he walked down the streets of the city without his clerical collar on he could walk right by parishioners who knew him well and they would not notice him. This made him feel that he was real to many people only in terms of his clerical collar and the priestly functions it represented, and not as a human being.

When people relate to us in terms of our profession rather than who we are as people, we speak of the relationship as a "transference." Transference is a term that has arisen from the practice of psychotherapy to denote the special relationship that develops between the therapist and the client.

The word is not used with a precise meaning. For instance, the transference may simply refer to the rapport that must exist between two people for psychotherapy to take place. It may also refer to the expectations that the client brings into therapy and places upon the therapist. In certain cases the transference may include projections from the client onto the therapist of archetypal images (such as that of the savior or healer). We also speak of the counter-transference, which refers to what the therapist is bringing into the relationship and places upon the client. Every transference is unique, but where there is a transference one person sees another person in a special way in terms of certain hopes, expectations, or images.

We all have transferences with other people. If you have fallen in love with someone, for instance, that relationship can be spoken of as a transference, for you have transferred to the object of your affections a certain archetypal image (as I have shown in my book *The Invisible Partners*). If you are ill and go to your doctor you almost certainly will bring to her your hopes and expectations, or perhaps even see the doctor in terms of the archetypal image of the savior or healer, which will make her much bigger in your eyes than an ordinary person. It is perfectly natural that such transferences should develop, and sometimes helpful too. For instance, if you transfer your hopes to the doctor, or see the doctor as the savior, this may help to inspire in you the attitudes of faith and confidence that you will need in order to speed your recovery. Just the same, to the extent that you have a transference on your doctor you will *not* see her in her purely human proportions. Looking at someone through the eyes of a transference makes that person appear different, just as things look different if you look at the world through dark glasses.

We have been discussing positive transferences, but

there is also such a thing as a negative transference when we project a negative image onto someone. For instance, the priest or doctor may be perceived as a kind of sorcerer, or as the conniving professional who is out to get your money, and the girl you have fallen in love with who seems to be a goddess can, under certain circumstances, suddenly appear to you as a witch. In fact it often happens that if a positive transference collapses, a negative transference takes its place.

If someone puts a transference on us we speak of "carrying" a transference. Like almost everything else, carrying a transference has its positive and its negative aspects. On the positive side, it sometimes facilitates the work to be done, helping create the special psychological atmosphere in which healing can progress, in the manner described in the case of the doctor. On the other hand, carrying a transference has two dangers: inflation and weariness.

If you are carrying a transference for someone it brings the danger that you may become puffed up about yourself. It is hard to have people see you as a god without beginning to think, on some secret level, that maybe you are some kind of a god. Therapists, priests, and doctors are especially vulnerable to this and may easily succumb to the notion that they are godlike and act accordingly. Such an inflated idea of ourselves can take place whether we recognize it or not. Even though we adopt a self-deceiving posture of Christian humility we may be inflated, for our egocentricity can be so subtle that our carefully cultivated humility only adds to our image of saintliness.

At first when we carry a transference for people it seems desirable because it is flattering, but sooner or later we experience it as a burden and it begins to tire us.

For one thing, to carry a transference means that some-thing has been handed to us that we are expected to live up to. It also means that if our all-too-human reality should break through and disrupt the transference, the person will see us in terms of a negative transference in-stead, and it is no fun to carry a negative transference for someone. Most of all, it wearies us to carry a transference because we are essentially carrying some of the psyche of other people that they need to find within themselves. It may help other persons for a while if they can park their savior image on us, but ultimately, unless they find that source of faith and hope in themselves, we wind up in a compulsive relationship in which we have to be God for someone. C. G. Jung once said that if he carried for some-one the projection of his or her creative side, he felt as though he was walking around with a corpse inside of him, because that creative side was dead to the person to whom it properly belonged as long as it was projected onto Dr. Jung.

In contrast to relationships that have a marked ele-ment of transference are the bulk of our ordinary human relationships. In these relationships people do not relate to us in terms of our profession, nor do they see us through the eyes of special hopes, expectations, or arche-typal images. Instead they see us and relate to us in a very human way, just as we are. To compensate for the fact that the ministering person will inevitably have many relationships in which a transference is involved, he must cultivate ordinary relationships as a counterbal-ance. He will need these relationships for at least three reasons.

First, we need ordinary human relationships because they nourish the soul. When there is a transference peo-ple tend to approve or disapprove of us in terms of whether or not we are fulfilling the expectations and images placed on us. In neither case are we genuinely loved or disliked for what we are. Eros, the quality of personal warmth and affection, is like a rare flower that can only develop to its finest in relationships that are devoid of the transference. The soul, which hungers for Eros, needs such relationships in order to find its proper nourishment. Eros occurs when we are related to people, as father, mother, husband, wife, or friend; it is here that our soul finds what it needs, and it is here that we can compensate for the dangers and difficulties of the professional relationships we must carry.

Second, we need these ordinary relationships because it is here that the most personal growth can take place. We must come up against other people who see us as we are if we are to properly develop. Sometimes others may love us, sometimes they may become angry at us, but if we are to grow as people we need these experiences. The love of such people can warm us, and their anger can show us our failings and shortcomings; we need both in order to develop our own capacity for relatedness and to become fully human.

As Adolf Guggenbuhl-Craig has shown in his fine book *Power in the Helping Professions,* people who serve the needs of others need ordinary human relationships in a special way. This is because members of the helping professions, including ministers of course, may be seduced into building up a life in which all their relationships are made via the transference. There is, then, no one to challenge them as people, no one whom they love and with whom they are vulnerable, no one with whom they can grow as human beings.

Third, ordinary relationships "coagulate" (think of it as solidify) the personality, and this is another reason why we need them. Transference relationships, as we have seen, have an element of illusion in them. After all, we are not savior, healer, goddess, or witch, but an ordinary human being. Yet we can hardly help but become inflated if enough people see us in terms of these powerful images. In ordinary relationships, however, we are brought down to earth (sometimes with a thud). This is why in such relationships we can become firm as personalities, that is, coagulated.

In order for a person to achieve a durable and solid personality he must recognize his dark side. In psychology we call this dark side the Shadow. The Shadow refers to the secondary personality within us that combines all of our unwanted qualities. For Christian people, who are trained to be nice, kind, loving, and unselfish, the Shadow is typically hostile, aggressive, conniving, ambitious, and self-serving. Yet in spite of the seemingly objectionable qualities that comprise the personality of this dark, other side of ourselves, the Shadow also serves a useful psychological purpose and is to be recognized, not rejected, as I have shown in Chapters Five, Six and Seven of my book *Evil: The Shadow Side of Reality.*

Without a connection to our dark side we are not real as people, and we also lack the vitality that the Shadow contains. Also, people who are cut off from their Shadow lack a sense of humor. Yet without the help of ordinary human relationships we will find it hard to learn what our Shadow is like, or how to come to terms with it. Only with the help of relationships with people whom we love, in which we may hurt them or fail them, can we be aware of our Shadow.

There is an old folk tale about a man who met the devil and made a bargain with him: if the devil would help him fulfill his ambitions he would sell the devil his shadow (in this case, his literal shadow, the dark outline of ourselves that can be seen when we stand in the light). The devil agreed, and the man let the devil walk off with his shadow. But then he discovered to his dismay that no one could see him! Without his shadow he was doomed to roam the earth as an invisible man. It is the same with us. Without a connection to our dark inner personality we are not real; we are not a solid personality, and cannot be seen for who we are.

The ministering person is tempted to try to live without a Shadow, and others will unwittingly assist in this devilish business because they do not want to see the ministering person's Shadow either; they want that person to stand only in the light and not have any darkness. If these are the only kinds of relationships we have, we become two-dimensional, going through life like cardboard people instead of real people. Without our dark side to help us become solid, three-dimensional personalities, we eventually lose touch with life's vitality, until even our most devoted transference relationships begin to notice that something has happened. That is when we need to turn to someone with whom we can be real in order to find our own reality and the energy for life.

7

Feeding the Soul

"Because he works with people in need, there is a particularly great drain on the energy of the ministering person."

Earlier we spoke of the work of helping others in terms of giving people blood transfusions. This is a good image, for it reminds us that the ministering person faces the danger of a severe energy drain in her work with people who are in need or distress. To help ourselves, we need to be aware of the energy drain that our work entails, and of the need for keeping the inner person strong and nourished.

Helping other people can be rewarding when we see the results of our efforts. To help a sick person get well, to assist a failing marriage to become strong again, to guide a person who is wandering in life, is a great satisfaction. However, not every case works out this way. It is not easy to help people under the best of circumstances, and when conditions are not favorable it may be almost impossible.

Sometimes you put energy into a person and are gratified to see him change for the better. He took the energy you gave him and used it to build up a more effective life and personality. But in other cases you can put energy into people, and when you see them again they are just as they were before. No matter how much energy you give them they never seem to change; they always require more from you.

If you have the plug in the sink and pour water into it, the water stays there and you can wash your face or clothes or do something else that is useful, but if the plug is missing, the water you pour into the sink will go down the drain and disappear. It is like this when you help people. Some people you can help, but other people do not seem to have any plug. Then when you pour energy into them it just disappears and everything is as it was before.

In such a situation it may be best to resign as the helping person. You have only so much energy to give, and you cannot pour it out endlessly or heedlessly. If your efforts are not bearing fruit, either that person cannot be helped or you are not the one to help him.

Ministering persons need to be able to recognize the people whom they cannot help. For instance, people who have fixed paranoid delusional systems cannot be helped by psychotherapy or spiritual counsel (except to a limited extent in certain cases, in conjunction with medication that must be administered by a psychiatrist). The psychopathic or sociopathic personalities also cannot be helped because they evidence no sense of moral values and have no motivation to change. Others who cannot be helped are those people who suffer from too grave a mental or character disorder. Persons in the ministry need to be able to recognize such people so that they will not spend their energy fruitlessly or entangle themselves in a pastoral situation that could be dangerous to them.

There are two other types of people who may take our energy who are not necessarily mentally ill, but who are unable or unwilling to use our help constructively.

The first type seems to lack sufficient life vitality. It is as though that person's inner fires burn low so that there is not enough energy in him to live life on his own. Such a person will be hard to help because there is not enough there to build on.

This does not mean that such a person cannot be helped to a degree. In psychotherapy such cases are well known, and psychotherapists do work with such people. Not many therapists like this kind of work, but they do it for two reasons. First, because they know if they put energy into that person it at least will help him to maintain a certain level in life. (For this reason such therapy is called "maintenance therapy.") Second, they do it because they get paid for doing it, and this represents a return on their output of energy. But not many religious professionals are going to get paid for their efforts, so it may be best to refer such draining cases to someone who will get paid. This may sound callous, but it is better than becoming exhausted and not having energy available for the people one can help.

The second kind of person who may drain us is the person whom Fritz Kunkel called the "Clinging Vine." The Clinging Vine is a person whose particular egocentric way of getting through life is to cling dependently to other people, or institutions, rather than stand on her own two feet. This person does not want to find her own strength; she wants to use the strength of others. Her posture is that she is very needy or very good or both. Her attitude is, "I am a very needy and/or good person; therefore you have to help me."

As we have seen, ministering people have trouble handling guilt, and as a result they are vulnerable to Clinging Vines because Clinging Vines make people feel guilty if they do not help them. The trouble is that Clinging Vines cannot be helped by other people. The more you try to help them, the more you confirm them in their clinging, dependent attitudes. They will positively refuse to stand on their own two feet, for if they did so they would have to give up their Clinging Vine attitude and pull their own oar in life.

The Clinging Vine differs from the person who lacks vitality because the latter seems under-endowed by nature, while the former could get well if she wanted to. In the Fifth Chapter of John's Gospel we have a good example of a Clinging Vine. Jesus was passing by the pool of Bethsaida. The sick and maimed gathered around this pool because periodically an angel troubled the water and the first person to reach the pool after the angel had troubled the water would be cured. One man had been by the pool for thirty-eight years but he still was not cured. Jesus knew this and said to him, "Do you want to be well again?" Instead of answering directly the man gave an excuse: "Sir, I have no one to put me into the pool when the water is disturbed; and while I am still on the way, someone else gets there before me." Then Jesus said something startling: "Get up, pick up your sleeping-mat and walk." The man was immediately cured, and walked away.

One would think that this man would be grateful, but he was not. To the contrary, as the story tells us, he did everything he could to get Jesus into trouble. The truth is that he resented being cured. He preferred to be a Clinging Vine and spend his life piteously by the side of the pool, and he was angry at Jesus for making that impossible any longer. Notice also that Jesus does not say something like, "Go your way; your faith has made you whole." Not to this man! Jesus cured him in spite of himself. We can only imagine that the Lord was feeling especially mischievous that day when he played such a trick on the man by the pool.

Jesus had the power to make this man well in spite of himself, but I do not think that many ministering persons will claim that kind of power to heal. This being the case, we need to think twice before bleeding ourselves to death trying to help such people. And in churches we *do* find such people, for religious institutions are excellent places for clinging.

The thought of refusing to help someone sits hard with ministering people. My very words, "We need to think twice before bleeding ourselves to death trying to help such people," may strike some as harsh, and hardly befitting a Christian attitude. But the truth is, as Fritz Kunkel once remarked, the only way to help a Clinging Vine is to withdraw all help. If what we want is to feel virtuous, to Star at being the good guy, the needed person, or the saintly and long-suffering helper, then go ahead and help the Clinging Vines! But if what we want is to see people get stronger, it is better if we stop helping entirely. If the Clinging Vine has exhausted all possibilities—and he does this in time because he wears people out—it is just possible that he may begin to help himself.

C. G. Jung once remarked that in psychotherapy the factor that is most influential is the relationship between the personality of the therapist and that of the client. In this relationship we hope that the more conscious and integrated personality of the therapist will affect the relatively disorganized personality of the client in such a way that the personality of the latter will be positively affected and he will begin to get better.

The same thing would be true of the pastoral and counseling relationships of the ministering person. But sometimes it works the other way around, for the personality of the client can affect the personality of the ministering person adversely. Then instead of the client's getting better, the minister gets worse. If you are a helping person and this begins to happen, you need to know that you cannot help. If someone is drowning and you can swim out and rescue him, well and good, but if someone is drowning and you know that if you try to rescue him you will drown too, you have to think twice before plunging into heroic action. Two drowned persons do not add up to one rescued person.

A therapist reported that the work he was doing with a young woman prone to dissociation and suicidal fantasies had begun to go badly. No matter how hard he tried to help her, she did not seem to be gaining in strength. Instead she began to phone him in the evenings, full of anxiety and fearfulness. She was often left alone due to the nature of her husband's work, and in her solitude she would have morbid, suicidal thoughts. The therapist dutifully and conscientiously would talk to her over the phone, but nothing he could say seemed to help, and when they terminated the phone conversation he was anxious and distraught from the effect of the talk and the fear that she might take her own life. This went on for some weeks, and the therapist began to notice neurotic reactions in himself. When the phone rang, for whatever reason, he found himself reacting with anxiety. After a phone conversation with his client his sleep would be disturbed. He found himself dreading to see her for appointments. It was not that he did not like her, for he did and he wanted to help her, but the truth was that instead of his client's condition getting better, he was getting worse.

One evening, after a particularly difficult phone call,

he knew that he had to do something about his situation. So he called her back and carefully and frankly explained to her that he was not helping her, that he himself was feeling bad, and that he had concluded that she must go to another therapist (he had one to recommend), or, if she felt she could not manage her life or control her suicidal impulses, that she should go to a hospital. This was not what she wanted to hear, but he himself immediately felt much stronger.

The story has an interesting conclusion. The young woman phoned the next day and asked for one more appointment, which was granted. When she came for her hour she worked hard on her problems, and asked for a second appointment, which was granted also. There were no more evening phone calls and no more reports of suicidal fantasies, and the woman promptly began to make a solid recovery.

So as it turned out, the therapist did not have to discontinue his work with his client, but he did have to take steps to protect himself. And it was exactly this action on his part that proved most helpful to the young woman.

This brings up a special problem for ministering persons who do counseling: should the counselee be asked to pay or not? If someone goes to see a professional psychotherapist there is no question about paying; of course the client pays, for that is how the therapist makes a living. There may be some grumbling, but it is expected. But when people see the religious professional they do not usually expect to pay, partly because the ministering person may be seen as above such worldly considerations, and partly because that person is, presumably, on a salary to do such work.

It may well be that we are on a salary, and that it would not be acceptable to either our church or our own code of ethics for us to take payment for pastoral counseling. But the fact remains that there is, generally speaking, a need on the part of the client to pay for the counseling he is receiving. There are good reasons for this. First, if the client does all the receiving and none of the giving, the relationship becomes unequal. This inequality creates guilt in the client, and a relationship in which he feels inferior. This proves to be inimical to growth. Second, if a person does not pay for his counseling, he is not likely to take it seriously. We think twice about going to counseling when we know we must pay for it. However, if it is free we go as much as we like, and as long as it does not hurt us in the pocketbook we do not have to work at it. Third, if someone pays for the counseling he receives from his minister, he is prevented from using that relationship for egocentric reasons. For instance, some people will seek out a minister for counseling rather than a psychiatrist, psychologist, marriage counselor, or other professional, precisely because it will not cost them anything, though of course they do not acknowledge this to the minister, and maybe not even to themselves. This kind of attitude is not conducive to personal growth, and will work against the success of the counseling.

All of these considerations make the matter of an exchange of money in pastoral counseling difficult. A practical solution might be this: if the person who comes for counseling is an attending and financially supporting member of the congregation, she has a right to a certain amount of the time of the paid religious professional on the staff. But if the counseling goes on for a long time, payment for it should be discussed, for now a disproportionate amount of the ministering person's time is being requested. If the person seeking counseling is not a supporting member of the church, payment for the counseling could certainly be discussed. If payment is decided upon, and the ministering person does not deem it appropriate to take the fee personally, the money can be paid into a Discretionary Fund or some other special church fund. The ministering person may find a discussion of such financial matters difficult, but he will also find that the proper resolution of this problem is an important part of the therapy.

He may also find that the counselee is relieved that the matter of payment has been brought up, for many people want to pay for their pastoral counseling or spiritual direction, and it helps them to have the matter openly discussed so that they know how to go about it.

The final antidote to the energy drain that comes from the work of helping people lies with the proper nourishment of the soul. It is the inner person who needs to be strong in order to do intense spiritual work year in and year out. An athlete who expends energy in running, swimming, or other forms of physically exhausting competition knows that periods of an intense output of energy must be balanced by periods of recuperation. Physical prowess is attained by a combination of physical striving, which brings the body to the point of maximum output and efficiency, with periods of rest, which allow the body to reorganize its energy, recoup its losses, and heal its hurts. So the spiritual athlete also needs to minister to her own inner self and fill the needs of her own soul in order to be fit for the next round of work. Spiritual energy must be replaced as well as physical energy.

This spiritual requirement is exemplified in the Bible in the many stories and images of food and eating. For instance, the people of Israel were nourished by God with manna as they wandered through the desert, and

Elijah, whom we will look at more closely in a later chapter, was fed by the ravens as he fled from Ahab and journeyed to Mount Sinai.

In the Gospels the image of food is on the center of the stage. "Man does not live on bread alone but on every word that comes from the mouth of God," Jesus declared to Satan when tempted by him to use his power to turn stones into bread. In this way Jesus made it clear that man needs food for the soul as well as for the body. And in the Lord's Prayer one of the central petitions is, "Give us this day our daily bread."

In John's Gospel Christ compares himself to the bread of heaven. He is a heavenly food come down from heaven to give life to the world. The disciples are admonished to "work for food that endures to eternal life, the kind of food the Son of Man is offering you." And Christ says of himself, "I am the bread of life. He who comes to me will never be hungry; he who believes in me will never thirst."

All of the Gospels agree on the importance of food for the soul. In fact, the most frequently told story in the Gospels is the story of the Feeding of the Multitude, which is found in all four Gospels and occurs a total of six times (in several variations). The theme is clear: there is a food from God that miraculously can nourish the souls of all humankind.

The story of the Feeding of the Multitude presages, of course, the story of the Eucharistic feast. In the final analysis, Christ on the Cross becomes the food for humankind, mediated through the Eucharistic feast. Even today in the Episcopal Church, as the body of Christ is given to the worshiper, the priest admonishes, "Feed on Him in your heart by faith, with thanksgiving."

Many persons who practice psychotherapy recognize the importance of being in some kind of therapy themselves. They know that their work with people's troubles has a certain tearing down effect on them, and they need to remain in touch with their own healing process. They know that they can become emptied by trying to help others become filled, and that they need to find soul-food in order to remain strong and protect themselves from the psychological hazards of their profession. So also ministering persons, whose calling it is to nourish and help others, need to find ways to nourish themselves in order to maintain their own spiritual strength and renew their energies. In a later chapter we will comment in more detail on some of the ways in which a person can find such nourishing spiritual food.

8

The Problem
of Egocentricity

"The ministering person deals with many people who come to her or the church not for solid spiritual food but for 'strokes.'"

We have already discussed what it means to give and receive strokes. We have seen that strokes are not genuine spiritual food, but, like candy, are temporary palliatives that make people feel better only for the moment. To want to receive strokes from the minister of the church instead of genuine spiritual nourishment is an example of egocentricity. On the other hand, to want to give strokes may also be an example of egocentricity.

This is what makes the matter of giving strokes such a problem for the ministering person: his own egocentricity is involved, as well as that of other people. This creates a problem that the ministering person cannot resolve unless he looks to himself to see where his egocentric need to give strokes feeds into the egocentric need of people to receive them.

We have referred several times to egocentricity or egocentric attitudes, and now is the time to look more deeply into the subject. Our guide will be Fritz Kunkel, whose name came up earlier. Kunkel explored in depth the origin and nature of egocentricity, and how the egocentric attitude betrays the purposes of God for the development of the individual. What follows is a simplification of the ideas that Kunkel elaborated in his books *How Character Develops* and *In Search of Maturity,* and which he used in his commentary on Matthew's Gospel, *Creation Continues.*

Kunkel believed that a child is born into the world with an innate capacity to love and trust other human beings. The child has, so to speak, a tribal mentality and looks upon others as a great tribe to which she belongs. In our culture, this instinctive trust is primarily directed to the parents (or parent substitutes). When this love and trust is met by maturity, love, and loyalty from the parents, there then springs up a connectedness between the child and the adults that Kunkel called the "We."

Where the We exists we have people who are connected together in such a way that they form a psychic unit; yet it is a non-egocentric association that in no way precludes the individual development and personalities of each member of the We. Suppose, for instance, that you took a trip with your family or a group of friends, and on your return someone asked you how your vacation was. You might reply, "Oh, we had a grand time." Your use of the word "we" would signify that on this trip you and your companions formed a psychic unit that embraced all the individuals in the group without nullifying their individuality.

Such is the ideal state into which the child is born, but of course there are no adults who are so conscious, loving, and loyal that they can offer the child the perpetual We-relationship for which the child is instinctively suited. Sooner or later the We is broken by the parents'

egocentric attitudes. This "Breach-of-the-We" precipi-
tates the child's own egocentricity which eventually becomes his own adult egocentric adaptation.

Egocentricity has one main concern: the desire to
defend the Ego at all costs. The egocentric attitude produces a personality that revolves around the Ego and directs a person's energies to the maintenance and defense
of the Ego. You could say that the egocentric person, instead of going out into the world to find genuine life,
spends most of his time building and defending the walls
of a castle. He reckons his castle as a place of defense and
security when, in fact, it is more like a prison.

The price a person pays for his egocentricity is the
sacrifice of the creative life, for life, in order to be creative, must be centered around the Real Self, not around
the Ego. The Real Self is the essential core of the personality out of which emerges our genuine personality, and
is the source of all creative living.

It is not that the Ego is inherently evil. When the
Ego assumes its proper role in the personality it is positive and creative because it is in contact with the Real
Self. Only when the Ego deviates from its proper function and purpose does it become the instrument of darkness. From the Christian point of view the egocentric
Ego is rebelling against the will of God, and deviating
from its God-ordained purpose in life, and this deviation
constitutes sin. But when the Ego is redeemed from its
egocentric posture and plays its proper role in life, it is
related to God and God's will.

For this reason, Kunkel felt that God tries to free us
from our egocentricity and lead us to the creative life.
This requires a developing consciousness on our part, including consciousness of our egocentric deviations, as
well as the kind of maturation that can only come

through carrying life's suffering properly. When this state of being is achieved we might say with St. Paul, "I live now not with my own life (that is, the egocentric Ego) but with the life of Christ (which, psychologically speaking, is the Real Self) who lives in me" (Gal. 2:20).

The egocentricity of the child, and later of the adult, may take one of several forms. Which form emerges depends on the basic nature of the child and the circumstances in which the child is raised. The important factors are the harshness or softness of the environment on the one hand, and the relative vitality, aggressiveness, and determination of the child on the other hand. The resulting combinations are four in number:

1. A child who lacks vitality and/or aggressiveness, or is overly sensitive, is raised in an environment that is soft, indulgent, and overly permissive. This is the pampered child.

2. A child who has considerable vitality and aggressiveness, and some talents to go with them, is raised in a soft, indulgent, and overly permissive environment. This is the admired child.

3. A child who lacks vitality and aggressiveness is raised in a harsh, brutal environment. This is the rejected, injured child.

4. A child who has a great deal of vitality and aggressiveness is raised in an environment that is harsh and brutal. This is the self-assertive, brutalized child.

Out of these four possible combinations come the four types of egocentricity that Kunkel calls the Clinging Vine, the Star, the Turtle, and the Nero (Tyrant).

We have already described the Clinging Vine to a certain extent, but at the risk of repetition let us look at this type again. This is the child who lacks drive and vitality, but finds herself with parents who create a soft, indulgent, non-demanding environment. The parents may think that they are being kind to the child by pampering her. In fact, their own egocentricity has led them to confuse softness and permissiveness with love, and their inability to confront their child with realistic expectations, or to let their child be confronted by the harshness of the world, springs from their subtle neglect of the child. Such egocentricity on the part of the parents creates the conditions for a corresponding egocentricity in the child, and the child, when she becomes a parent, will pass on her egocentricity in turn.

Later, as an adult, such a child will become a Clinging Vine who makes her way through life by clinging dependently to people, in the way we have already described. Her carefully cultivated posture of being very good or very needy is calculated to create the conditions she desires by evoking from other people enough sympathy, kindness or guilt, so they feel impelled to support her as she wants to be supported. Thus the Clinging Vine unconsciously plots to avoid standing on her own two feet.

The Star is the more vital child raised in the indulgent environment. This child finds herself the center of a world of indulgent and admiring parents. Perhaps these parents even satisfy their own unfulfilled ambitions by adulating their successful child. They think that this adulation of their child is love, and fail to see the egocentricity of their desire to have her be a star in their own crown. Nor do they see how, by pushing the child forward, they are avoiding the need to deal with their own development and fulfillment.

The Star may star at all sorts of things. She may become an all-A student (and be thrown into despair if she gets a B), or the best singer in the choir (and be furious if someone else is chosen to sing the solo), or a Star at being very "good" (and consequently finding it necessary to repress her Shadow). Whatever wins the required admiration and approval will do, so naturally she picks that activity at which she is best and most pleases others. As an adult, this person continues to strive for the center of the stage. Her consuming need is for admiration, and much of her energy goes into seeing that she is a properly adulated person.

The Turtle is the child who lacks the necessary vitality or aggressiveness to cope with a harsh environment, or who is extremely sensitive and so is easily overwhelmed by hurts.

The harshness of the environment may come from parents who are brutal, rejecting, and tyrannical, or from a harsh social environment (like a ghetto). The harshness may be obvious, such as a child who is beaten by his parents. Or it may be quite subtle. Everything may seem to be perfect, with a beautiful home and polite parents, but there may be a subtly damaging psychological environment with which the child cannot cope. Psychologist Gregory Bateman, for instance, has described the "double-bind." This occurs when no matter what the child does he loses; if he does one thing the parents disapprove, but if he does the other they also disapprove. When such conditions exist there is a psychological cruelty going on that is just as damaging to the child as the overt cruelty of harsh physical punishment.

The response of the Turtle is to withdraw, to seek shelter by removing himself psychologically from a life that has become too dangerous. We call this type the Turtle for obvious reasons. A turtle is a weak and defenseless animal that gets along in life only because it can withdraw into the protection of a heavy shell. Similarly, the Turtle person feels weak and vulnerable, and gets along by retreating into a shell so that no one can hurt him.

As an adult, the Turtle's posture is, "Don't expect anything of me; don't make me come out of my shell and take risks or become vulnerable; don't demand courage from me." The Turtle often wins our sympathy for he is, in fact, an injured person. Nevertheless we have to call him egocentric too, for the defensive posture of his Ego defeats the purposes of life, and his main efforts are directed at self-protection rather than creative living. (In the Gospels he is illustrated by the man in the Parable of the Talents who was given one talent, but buried it in the ground so that he could not lose it and be criticized when his Master returned.)

Finally there is the Nero, named after the ruthless Roman emperor who was the first to persecute the Christians. The Nero or Tyrant, like the Turtle, is also exposed to a harsh environment, but, being more aggressive, he solves the problem by becoming more brutal and ruthless than the tyrannical people around him. He deals with his psychological difficulties by pushing his way to the top and dominating others. As long as he is in a position of power he feels secure and confident, but should he lose his power, he feels annihilated.

As an adult, a well-endowed Nero might become a Stalin; such a person thinks nothing of exterminating other people in order to maintain his power position. Only his paranoid fears betray an inner weakness which his otherwise dominating nature successfully conceals. If he is not as talented as a Stalin, he might have to settle for the life of a minor bureaucrat who tyrannizes helpless people by telling them that their forms are not filled out correctly. Or he might become a tyrannical teacher, military officer, policeman, criminal, or parish priest.

We have said that the egocentricity of the child is started when the egocentricity of the parents breaks the original We. This seems to place all the blame on the parents. In fact we are reminded of the saying quoted in the Old Testament, "The fathers have eaten sour grapes and the children's teeth are set on edge" (Ezek. 18:2, KJV; cf. Jer. 31:29). But it does no good to blame our parents for our egocentric patterns. They had their parents too, and these people had their parents. Egocentricity is like original sin in that it is the inevitable human condition. So our task is not to blame our parents (which is only another form of egocentricity), but to struggle with our own psychology, assume responsibility for our own egocentric deviations, and strive to help God achieve His purpose in our lives.

Of course this presentation of Kunkel's analysis of egocentricity is much too brief and schematic. Like all psychological concepts, these concepts are only valid insofar as they help us think creatively about ourselves and our relations to others. They cannot be followed slavishly, for every person is an individual, and our unique psychology never exactly fits within the boundaries of broad psychological descriptions.

For this reason not many people will fit exactly into these categories. For instance, some people were exposed as children to an environment that was sometimes soft and indulgent and sometimes harsh and brutal. (Perhaps the child had an indulgent mother and a cruel father, or the other way around.) When this occurs there will be two different egocentric adapatations, one coming into operation under certain conditions, and the other under different conditions.

We may also have one egocentric adaptation in one area of life and another in a different area. For instance, a businessman may be a dominating Nero at the office, but in situations that call for personal intimacy he may be a Turtle who runs and hides. Under certain circumstances we may also change from one egocentric form to another. For instance, a Star who is defeated in his attempts to win adulation may revert to being a Clinging Vine, and a defeated Nero readily turns into a craven Turtle (which is why bullies are so often also cowards).

Nor should we be confused by the seeming similarities of these types. For instance, the Star and the Nero sometimes look alike, but the Star seeks adulation and the Nero seeks power. The Nero will be satisfied to remain in the background, and even to be actively disliked, as long as he has power, while the Star does not care for power as much as he seeks glory. A Turtle and a Clinging Vine also may look alike, but the former retreats from life into a shell, while the latter goes out to meet people, but only to enlist them in the service of his clinging dependency.

It is also true that few people are purely egocentric. There is almost always a mixture of the egocentric and the genuine in our personality. Sometimes we may exhibit the qualities of the Real Self and live creatively and courageously, and sometimes our egocentric side may take over. In a garden the weeds spring up right next to the flowers and they grow side by side. So it is in our personality; the desirable and undesirable qualities are not far apart, but develop next to each other.

Finally, we need to point out the effect of egocen-

tricity on other people, Egocentric people have a negative effect on others; they tire us, bore us, seduce us, or
frighten us. In contrast, people who live more from the
genuine Self have a positive effect on others and win our
genuine admiration. Even if their positive qualities are
not recognized at the time, because we are too short-
sighted to see them or too threatened by them, later on
they will be recalled.

Churches, like other organizations, have their share
of egocentric people, and ministering people have no im-
munity against egocentricity in spite of their protesta-
tions of faith in God. In fact, many ministering people
may have an overdose of egocentricity, and mingled
with their sincere desire for a God-centered and sacrifi-
cial life, they may have their egocentric reasons for want-
ing to live the life of a religious professional.

Clinging Vines may find the church a splendid institution to which they can cling. Persons who would be
fired in a minute from a business because of laziness or
inefficiency may find lifelong toleration in the church
which, with an overly soft and indulgent attitude, puts
up with inferior qualities.

The Star, too, may find the church a splendid place.
If he has gifts as a preacher, is personable with an effective manner of making people feel important, or is
unusually good at striking a saintly, loving, or concerned-
with-others pose, he may find the church a splendid
stage on which to win the desired adulation.

A well-established Turtle will usually find a hospital
more to her liking than a church, but Turtles also have
been known to crawl within the shelter of mother
church, finding there a protection against the hostile
world which they fear is all around them.

Neros probably wind up in churches less than Stars,

but when they do they can have a glorious time being the big frog in the little puddle, especially in churches that give their priests tenure (like the Episcopal Church). In such denominations a Nero may be entrenched against his enemies and become the tyrant of the parish. True, in dominating the parish he wins the dislike of many people, but a Nero, unlike a Star, is not affected by disapproval as long as his need for power is achieved.

Now clearly a ministering person cannot serve both God and his egocentricity. So it is extremely important for their spiritual development that ministering people ferret out their particular forms of egocentricity and try to do something about them. Kunkel describes how this can be accomplished, but to repeat here what he has said would go beyond the scope of this book. Suffice it to say that one place to begin is to notice our response to the demands of people for strokes. If we find ourselves meeting this demand, why are we doing it? Are we Clinging Vines who have a secret alliance with other Clinging Vines? (You support my need and I will support yours.) Or are we Stars who know that giving people strokes is a certain way to win approval and admiration? (Again, you scratch my back and I'll scratch yours.) Or are we Neros who would ordinarily spurn giving people strokes, but are doing so now because it is a way to achieve eventual domination? How about Turtle? Turtle will find it hard to compete in the game of giving strokes. His defensive posture will make it hard for him to emerge enough from his shell to offer people what they need. But his egocentricity will show forth in his envy of those who can.

So the egocentricity of ministering persons and the egocentricity of the people whom they serve may join together in an unholy alliance. But sooner or later the system collapses. It takes a great deal of energy to maintain our egocentricity. Only the creative life brings us vital energy for living; the egocentric life drains energy from us. As the years go on it becomes harder and harder to maintain our egocentric posture successfully, as its satisfactions and reassurances are only temporary, and sooner or later we will burn out.

Fortunately, our Christian tradition helps us. Jesus once said, "Whosoever will come after me, let him deny himself, and take up his cross, and follow me" (Mk. 8:34, KJV). From the viewpoint of a religious psychology, to take up one's own cross means to take up the task of becoming a whole person. The cross is a place of death and eventual rebirth. What must die is the egocentric Ego. What rises is the new Ego, related to the Creative Self. This is why C. G. Jung once remarked that the emergence of the Self is always the defeat of the Ego. What is defeated is our egocentricity, and though we may fear and shun the psychological life crisis that will bring this about, there is nonetheless salvation within it. This theme is like a thread running through all of Christianity, the theme expressed by Jesus when He said that he who loses his life will find it. So the loss of the egocentric life is the discovery of the genuine Self, and the Christian images point the way through.

9

The Face We Put On

"The ministering person must function a great deal of the time on his 'persona.'"

We have already seen that the effort to maintain a persona can rob the ministering person of energy. Part of the difficulty is that we are not always aware when we are functioning through the persona. It can become so automatic to assume a persona when we go to work that we begin to think we are the person we pretend to be. The first step in dealing with this problem is to recognize when we are being genuine and when we are meeting other people through a mask. This may take some self-study. It may prove valuable to have a good spiritual director or therapist help us recognize our genuine self and our persona-self. In some cases group therapy may also be of value since other members of the group may demand that we be genuine with them; they are not likely to be impressed with the persona that people with a religious vocation so easily adopt.

There are other small ways by which we can help ourselves. For instance, one of the tasks of most clergy is to shake hands with people at the door after the worship service. This almost requires that we use our persona, for no one can greet several hundred people and say something pleasant to each one without using a persona. However, we do not have to make the problem worse than it is. We can say "Good morning" to people rather than "How are you?" The latter implies that we are really interested in how they are. With several hundred people waiting to speak to us, it is not likely that we are really interested in hearing how someone is. The simpler greeting, "Good morning," avoids this problem. More importantly, it reminds us of the need we have to avoid a persona as much as is possible in such a collective situation.

We have also mentioned that in addition to assuming a persona for ourselves other people may hand us a persona. There is a good story about this in Luke's Gospel in which Jesus was handed a persona by a member of one of the leading families of the community. What Jesus did under these circumstances is instructive:

> A member of one of the leading families put this question to him, "Good Master, what have I to do to inherit eternal life?" Jesus said to him, "Why do you call me good? No one is good but God alone" (Lk. 18:18–19).

The wealthy man handed Jesus the persona of being good, and Jesus handed it right back. Notice that he did this before he answered the man's question; he made it the first order of business. Jesus was not going to be burdened with the task of fulfilling this man's idea of being good; he handed it back to the man so that he could be himself.

Another interesting part of this story is what is *not* said at the end. When Jesus tells the man that if he wants eternal life he must sell all his wealth, give to the poor,

and come and follow him, the man walks away sorrowful-
ly, for he is not willing to do this. What we do *not* read is
that Jesus ran down the street after him pleading with
him to change his mind. Had Jesus been a modern
clergyman he might have gone after the man and said
something like, "Oh, you must come back. You are an
important person and we need you terribly. If you don't
want to give up all you have, at least give us a generous
donation and we will make you a member of the Vestry."
The name of the game is clear: generous strokes to the
wealthy man in return for a donation. Church buildings
get built this way, but not the kingdom of God.

The story of Jesus and Simon the Pharisee, which we
find in Luke 7:36–50, is also a helpful example. Jesus is
having a meal with one of the Pharisees when a woman
enters who is known to be a sinner. Evidently Jesus has
done something to help her, and the woman is so grateful that she washes Jesus' feet with her tears and dries
them with her hair. Simon the Pharisee thinks to himself,
"If this man were a prophet, he would know who this
woman is that is touching him and what a bad name she
has." Jesus, aware of what he is thinking, then asks him a
question: Suppose two men owed a creditor a debt, one a
large debt and one a small debt, and then the creditor
forgave them both. Which man would love him more?
Of course Simon has to reply that the man to whom a
great debt was forgiven would love him more. Then Jesus says:

> "Simon, you see this woman? I came into your house,
> and you poured no water over my feet, but she has
> poured out her tears over my feet and wiped them
> away with her hair. You gave me no kiss, but she has
> been covering my feet with kisses ever since I came

in. You did not anoint my head with oil, but she has anointed my feet with ointment. For this reason I tell you that her sins, her many sins, must have been forgiven her, or she would not have shown such great love."

Then he concludes with what must be the most paradoxical statement in the Gospels:

"It is the man who is forgiven little who shows little love."

What are we to do, lead evil lives so that we may be forgiven and thus learn to love? That may be going too far. But certainly we must lose the persona in order to face who we are and learn to love, and this is what the woman did in this story. On the other hand, Simon, while a Star at righteousness, able to live without blame in the eyes of others with the perfected persona of the Pharisee, could not really love.

The collective pressure on us as ministering persons to conform to a persona is just as great as the collective pressure to be "righteous" must have been upon Simon the Pharisee. In his book *Power in the Helping Professions,* previously mentioned, Adolf Guggenbuhl-Craig expresses this succinctly in these words:

... with the clergyman it is frequently the members of his congregation who involuntarily activate his dark brother. They exert considerable pressure on him to play the hypocrite. Doubt is the companion of faith. But no one wants to hear doubt expressed by a clergyman; we all have doubts enough of our own. Thus the priest often has no alternative but to be the hypocrite now and again, to hide his own doubts and to mask a momentary inner emptiness with high-flown words. If his character is weak, this can become a habitual stance.

A man of God in the ideal sense must bear witness to his faith by his actions. He cannot prove what he preaches. He is expected to provide by his own behavior a foundation for the faith which he represents. And this opens the door to another of the clergyman's dark brothers—the one who wishes to present himself to the world (and to himself) as better than he really is.

Of all the problems the ministering person faces that we have mentioned so far, perhaps the problem posed by the persona is the most important, for it strikes at the heart of our spiritual development. The main attack Jesus made on the evils of his time was not against stealing, sexual sins, or even violence, but against hypocrisy, that is, identification with the persona so we are no longer genuine people. This attack was mainly directed against the Pharisees, and this is why he made so many enemies and was crucified. Since the ministering person functions in a role in which she is handed a persona by the persons she serves, she is in danger of losing herself. But if we lose ourselves, we will also lose our energy. We will become like a watch that has lost its mainspring because we will have lost contact with our genuine Self, the Center of our being.

This problem may not seem of paramount importance in the beginning of our professional lives, for in the first part of life the Ego is in the ascendancy and shines like the sun at midday. Then we suppose we can continue indefinitely as we are, even though the life of the Ego is based upon the persona and not upon a relationship with our genuine, inner Center. But as youth passes into middle age the Ego begins to weaken, and if it is separated from the genuine part of the personality it will become more and more empty. Meanwhile, the real energy of the personality will accumulate in the unconscious, activating the Shadow, and setting up a state of inner opposition to an Ego that is so identified with the persona that it is becoming increasingly two-dimensional and stale. The result will be anxiety, despondency, and lack of creativity.

But if the ministering person is especially exposed because of his profession to the hazards of identification with the persona, he is also in a better position than many people to become aware of his spiritual problem, since the Gospels teach him about it and show him the way through. The very difficulty we face as ministering persons also creates a unique opportunity for self-knowledge and spiritual growth. And in the final analysis, this is the solution to the problem.

10

Elijah's Problem

"The ministering person may become exhausted by failure."

We have seen how debilitating a sense of failure can be to the ministering person. This is not hard to understand. If someone has worked for years, only to conclude that he is a failure, his morale can sink so low that it will be difficult for him to carry on. In these days, in which many churches are shrinking in size and influence, it is not hard for a ministering person to conclude that he has failed. A negative mood about himself and his work can then possess him.

When we contemplate failure we need to ask three questions: Are we failing because of some fault of our own? Are we failing because we are in a situation in which we cannot possibly win? Are we really failing or do we only think we are failing because we are measuring success by the wrong standards?

If we think we are failing because of some fault in ourselves, we may have to work harder on our personal development. This is a situation in which we will probably need the assistance of a skilled spiritual director or therapist. It is almost impossible to see ourselves without talking with another person trained in matters of psychology and of the spirit, and it is almost impossible to walk the spiritual path alone. At some point everyone needs a companion on the way, someone with whom we can share openly and honestly, whom we can trust to hold our confidences, and who we know will not judge us no matter what dark corners of our personalities we reveal.

We need not be ashamed to seek such help. In fact, to seek help from others is a sign in itself of health; the person who is unable to share her soul with another person is more likely to be really ill. The very nature of our work as pastors almost dictates that at some point in our ministries we need to work with another person on our own soul, for no one can lead another person in the path of spiritual development if she has not gone down that path herself, and no one can be a guide to the soul of another if she has not submitted to her own need for such a guide.

In our day, for some strange reason, the church has abdicated the care of souls to secular professions. But there now seems to be a growing awareness in the church of the need for religious persons skilled in the care of the soul. At the same time, there are also many dedicated therapists who stand outside of the church who are nevertheless sensitive spirits who can be helpful. One can almost always find the right person to help if the need and the will are there.

Are we fighting a losing battle? In the 1950's and 1960's it was easy to have a growing congregation; it was "in the air" to attend church, the popular thing to do. Now it seems to be reversed, especially with the mainline denominations. Clergy are often painfully aware of their shrinking congregations and inadequate parish and diocesan budgets. Those churches that are increasing in size often seem to be the ones that offer people the security of a rigid belief system, or to have as their pastor a person who is able to put on a spectacular display which others are unable to emulate.

Of course this situation varies from one parish to another. Some parishes are more strategically located than others, and some have a more vital spirit; these parishes may grow even in a general spiritual climate that is unfavorable to church growth. But other parishes may be located in places where the social situation is deteriorating. Or they may be parishes that have exhausted themselves, and are now made up of determined but narrow people who partly keep the shell of the parish alive and partly keep it from growing. Such a parish is like a tree on a rocky mountain cliff that is half dead and half alive, clinging to life but unable to grow any further. In such a situation it may be impossible to improve things significantly no matter who we are or what efforts we exert. To flagellate ourselves with self-recrimination in such an impossible situation would be like blaming ourselves because we cannot keep the tide from running out.

This brings us to the most important question of all: What constitutes failure in the ministry? So far we have been measuring success or failure in terms of the size of a congregation and its financial affluence; if the number of persons attending services increases and the budget grows, then surely we must be succeeding. Anxiously we examine the church service record at the end of the year to see if our statistics show that such "growth" has taken place. We can hardly help but be impressed with ourselves if our congregation appears to be flourishing and our budget increasing, and, conversely, feel diminished and unimportant if it is not. In the former case we hold our head high among our clergy brothers and sisters; in the latter case we may look enviously upon the seemingly successful person whose congregation is "on the way up."

The fact is that success in spiritual matters is difficult to measure. An increase in the size and financial affluence of a congregation is a handy measure of something, but it may not measure spiritual success. Indeed, the "successful" church may not be serving God's purposes at all; it may be serving the purposes of human egocentricity.

We have already discussed the problem of egocentricity, and observed how keenly people are interested in strengthening and perpetuating their egocentric defenses and egocentric adaptation to life. We have also observed how anything that threatens our egocentricity is vigorously resisted, and anything that supports our egocentricity is welcomed. One thing that supports egocentricity is joining oneself with other people in an association dedicated to the mutual support of each other's egocentric needs. Many groups function for the secret purpose of doing just this, and people flock to join such groups in anticipation of feeling more secure. Fritz Kunkel called this kind of a group "the Associated Egos." Any person who is able to develop and promote such a group is going to be a success—measured in egocentric and worldly terms.

Of course, not all large churches are egocentric, nor is a small congregation necessarily genuinely spiritual. Genuine spiritual growth and power in a church cannot necessarily be measured by its size, for God's measure is not man's measure.

When Samuel was looking for the man God would choose to succeed Saul as King of Israel he was led to the house of Jesse. Here Samuel thought that God would surely choose Jesse's older and impressive son Eliab as the future king, and not the youthful David, but when Samuel questioned God about Eliab, God replied, "Take no notice of his appearance or his height for I have rejected him; God does not see as man sees; man looks at appearances but Yahweh looks at the heart" (1 Sam. 16:7).

It is quite extraordinary what people will do for an organization that helps them maintain their egocentricity, which is why such an organization succeeds in terms of size and influence. And of course the leader of such a group is having his own egocentricity supported. Such a person is usually a Star or a Nero, and the success of his organization suits his egocentric needs perfectly. Because of this he has a great deal of energy for his work, and is a dedicated believer in what he is doing (repressing his inner doubts by projecting them onto outsiders). Such enthusiasm is contagious and attracts more people to him. In this way, leader and followers join together in a group, institution, or enterprise, which may protest that it is dedicated to some noble cause, but in reality is dedicated to their Egos. The true nature of their organization, of course, they keep secret—especially from themselves, for there is usually just enough genuineness in such people to horrify them if they saw clearly what they were actually doing.

So when we feel we are failing in our ministry we need to look closely and objectively at our situation. Are we really failing as completely as we think? Are we failing at all? No one succeeds one hundred percent of the time, of course, but is our batting average as low as our negative inner voices tell us? As we try to answer these questions we must remember that God is interested in individual people transformed into His sons and daughters, and not in how many are in the group. Jesus reminds us, "Enter by the narrow gate, since the road that leads to perdition is wide and spacious, and many take it; but it is a narrow gate and a hard road that leads to life, and only a few find it" (Mt. 7:13). Jesus uses the image of the narrow road because only one person at a time can pass down a narrow road. This is why spiritual "success" is measured in individuals, and the sum total may never be large.

We need not disparage our work because our success is with the few and not the many, for it is the gifted, developed, conscious, God-related individual who transforms the world. Out of the masses of people in the Civil War one man stands out—Abraham Lincoln. Out of the caldron of the ancient Near East one personality shines forth: that of Jesus himself. The ancient Chinese wisdom book, the *I Ching,* reminds us that the thoughts of one person who is in the right place and who is right with himself are heard a thousand miles away.

The story of Elijah in Chapters 18 and 19 of the First Book of Kings deals so profoundly with the problem of failure that it is a fitting way to conclude this chapter. Elijah won a great victory over the priests of Baal on Mount Carmel when his sacrifice to Yahweh was consumed by fire from heaven even though it had been drenched with water, and the terrible drought Yahweh had sent came to an end as a consequence of Elijah's prayers. But this victory was followed by a defeat so total that it sent Elijah retreating into the wilderness disheartened and bewildered, for Queen Jezebel, enraged at Elijah's destruction of her priests, hounded him unmercifully, renewed her persecution of Yahweh, and drove Elijah out of the land of Israel, an isolated and homeless refugee.

Wandering by himself in the desert Elijah falls into such a state of despair that he wishes he were dead. "Yahweh," he declares, "I have had enough. Take my life; I am no better than my ancestors." Elijah is burned out. He has exerted his best efforts, but, in spite of the immense energy he put out, all has apparently been lost. Now, totally exhausted, he only wants death, convinced that he is a failure and no better at doing Yahweh's work than the unsuccessful people who have preceded him.

However, Yahweh is unimpressed with Elijah's sense of failure because He does not see the situation as man sees it; He sees it from His divine perspective. So He sends His angel to rouse Elijah, feed him, and set him on his way on a long journey to Mount Sinai. Elijah travels many, many days and finally ascends the flank of the sacred mountain to a cave. Here he enters and huddles in a dark corner. He has undertaken a pilgrimage, in the sense that we discussed in an earlier chapter, and now, like an American Indian on a Vision Quest, he waits for a manifestation of the divine will.

There then ensues a dialogue between God and Elijah. God asks the prophet, "What are you doing here, Elijah?" And the discouraged prophet tells Him his story: how the sons of Israel have deserted Yahweh, how his work has failed, and now, he says, "I am the only one left, and they want to kill me."

God then tells Elijah that he should return to the land of Israel, and he is to anoint new people to be royalty and leaders in place of Ahab and Jezebel. Most important, He informs Elijah that not everyone has lost faith in Him, for there are seven thousand people who have not bent down the knee to Baal nor kissed Baal's idols. Elijah, his heart renewed, his sense of failure overcome, returns to Israel and completes his work.

This story illustrates many of the points we have made. It shows how a sense of failure can consume our energy and leave us depleted. It also shows that our feeling that we have failed may be a mistake: God did not think that Elijah had failed; He was impressed that there were seven thousand who were faithful to Him and reckoned this more than enough to continue the work. And Elijah did continue the work, but only because he had been able to talk with God. That is, his exhausted Ego had found a way to contact the source of renewal, for in his pilgrimage to Mount Sinai, and in his dialogue with God, Elijah's vital energies were replenished. So Elijah illustrates both the problem of the Exhausted Ego, and the possibility of the renewal of the Ego, and it is to this that we now turn.

11

The Problem
of the Exhausted Ego

The story of Elijah is about an Ego that has become exhausted. Elijah suffers from more than the chronic depression that is characteristic of Burnout; his is an exhaustion so complete that only the pilgrimage to Mount Sinai and the personality-reorienting dialogue with God can cure him.

The problem of Burnout and the problem of the Exhausted Ego are not entirely dissimilar. Burnout can lead to exhaustion, and where we find the Exhausted Ego the problem of Burnout is also sure to be there. We can liken them to first cousins—two clearly related problems, yet each one somewhat distinct from the other. The problem of Burnout is largely task-oriented and, by definition, stems from the wearing out of one's work. The problem of the Exhausted Ego is more fundamental, for it revolves around the wearing out of a person's entire Ego orientation.

One might suppose that a ministering person would not be subject to the problem of the Exhausted Ego, that such a person would be so in touch with God, and the satisfactions of a life in which one person labors for others

86

out of love, that the Ego would always be buoyant. But such is not the case. To the contrary, a life in which love and morality predominate has a tiring quality to it because it revolves around real relationships and requires the effort of caring. As Adolf Guggenbuhl-Craig has pointed out in his book *Eros on Crutches,* "Every real relationship is tiring; relationship requires an effort. Actually, anyone who is guided in his activity by Eros or the ersatz Eros, morality, is always a little tired." So the problem of Ego exhaustion is as likely to occur to the ministering person as it is to anyone else.

The problem of the Exhausted Ego is further complicated because it is almost always accompanied by the wearing out of what Jung called "the superior function." Jung saw that people differed from each other according to which of four psychological functions were most natural to them. He called these functions thinking, feeling, sensation and intuition. Actually, each person has all four of them as part of his personality, but one of them, which is the superior function, is strongest and comes most naturally. Two others are weaker and are used more awkwardly, and one, the so-called "inferior function," represents the psychological area in which one is least adapted.

It is not necessary for us to go into the details of Jung's theory of types. I have included a brief chapter on it in my books *The Kingdom Within* and *Between People,* and several other books are available describing this typology in detail. For now it is enough to know that each person is endowed by nature with certain capabilities and certain weaknesses. When we use those capacities that are the most natural to us we are rewarded by approval, more financial success, and the satisfaction of achieving. Naturally, then, in the course of its development the Ego identifies with its strong points, builds up an Ego out of them, and uses them in making a life for itself. Of course the capacities in us that are weaker are shunned, as are those areas of life that would require them.

So a person who is gifted with the ability to think analytically and logically might become a scientist or philosopher; a person with abundant feeling might involve himself with other people and their lives; someone gifted with the awareness of the concrete details of life might become an efficient secretary or a biologist; and another person who is intuitive might become a poet, psychologist, or artist. The scientist is likely to feel awkward in the realm of poetry, the poet may fail completely when it comes to fixing the plumbing in the house, the feeling type of person may be frightened in an algebra class, and the one skilled in logic may feel defeated in emotional relationships. It is natural that we utilize our superior gifts and make a life out of them, for then life works best for us.

It works best, that is, for a while. But eventually these superior psychological functions begin to wear out. Good though they are, we use them up, and as we use them up they lose their meaning. The energy goes out of them, and then energy goes out of us. This process may take a long time, and for this reason the problem of the Exhausted Ego is typically (though not necessarily) a gradually growing problem of middle or advancing years. In our youth the superior talents are filled with energy and consequently filled with meaning. We use them to achieve success and make our way in the world, and this gives the Ego energy. But by the time we reach thirty-five or forty or fifty the energy in the superior function may be wearing down. We have now lived the life of scientist, parent, psychologist, or teacher, and there is no longer any meaning for us in this activity. This is a dangerous point. The Ego may become exhausted. If it becomes sufficiently exhausted it may collapse entirely, or a person's vitality may gradually fade until the person disappears, perhaps through an early death.

When a life situation is as typical as this one, we can expect to find stories, legends, and myths that deal with it, for typical human problems find spontaneous expression in mankind's art, literature, and imagination. We have already looked at one such story: the tale of the Handless Maiden, in which the miller, whose mill is no longer productive, renews his business by selling his daughter to the devil. This story tells us how *not* to solve the problem of the Exhausted Ego: we are not to perpetuate mechanically the old state of affairs at the price of our own feminine soul. There are many other stories that describe the problem and also suggest a possible solution. We will look at some of these.

But first a word of caution. Notice that I said these stories "suggest a possible solution." No story, and no book, can do more than point out the general direction in which we as individuals may have to move to solve the problem of the Exhausted Ego because each solution to the problem is entirely individual. We may know a fair amount about how the problem of the Exhausted Ego can be solved, but we do *not* know how this problem can be solved for any particular individual. That solution must always be discovered by that person, and worked out in terms of that person's individual psychology and individual life. For this reason, the most helpful stories and ideas can tell us where we might find the path that will take us to renewal, but that is all. From there on we must find and walk that path ourselves, make our own discoveries, and have our own inner and outer adventures.

Let us begin with *Faust*, Goethe's famous poetic drama that tells of the plight of Professor Faust and his attempts to solve the dilemma by making an agreement with the devil.

Hail Professor Faust! He knows everything that can be known. He has read all the books that are worth reading. He is the learned man par excellence, the most renowned professor in the land, a man who, at the age of fifty, is at the pinnacle of his career and is surrounded by admiring students and envious colleagues. But he cannot stand it. He cannot bear himself or his life. He feels so desperate that he is at the point of suicide. His work no longer means anything to him, his learning does not tell him what he now needs to know, he has no further ambitions to keep him in this world. The opening lines of the drama tell the story:[1]

> I've read, alas! through philosophy
> Medicine and jurisprudence too,
> And, to my grief, theology
> With ardent labor studied through.
> And here I stand with all my lore,
> Poor fool, no wiser than before!
> I'm Master, I'm Doctor, and with my reading
> These ten years now I have been leading
> My scholars on wild-goose hunts, out
> And in, cross-lots, and round about—
> To find that nothing can be known!

---

[1]Translation by Charles E. Passage in Bobbs-Merrill publication. See Bibliography.

This burns my very marrow and bone.
I'm shrewder, it's true, than all the tribes
Of Doctors and Masters and priests and scribes;
Neither doubts nor scruples now can daunt me,
Neither hell nor devils now can haunt me—
But by the same token I lose all delight.
I don't pretend to know anything aright.
I don't pretend to have in mind
Things I could teach to improve mankind.
Nor have I lands nor treasure hoards,
Nor honors and splendors the world affords;
No dog would want to live this way!

. . . . .

Am I still in this prison stall?
Accursed, musty hole-in-the-wall,
Where the very light of heaven strains
But dully through the painted panes!

. . . . .

Do you still wonder why your heart
Is choked with fear within your breast?
Why nameless pain checks every start
Toward life and leaves you so oppressed?
Instead of Nature's living sphere
Wherein God placed mankind of old,
Brute skeletons surround you here
And dead men's bones and smoke and mold.

(Lines 354–417)

Faust's plight is the plight of an Ego that has exhausted itself, of a man who has used his primary function until it no longer has the power to bring him any
satisfaction. In the case of Professor Faust this function is
thinking, but his good intellect, once the light of his life,

no longer holds any meaning for him. The situation is serious, for under such circumstances life loses its color, and could come to an end entirely. Where can Faust turn to find new life?

To answer this question Goethe created one of the more remarkable characters of literature: the wily, cunning, humorous Mephistopheles, special agent of the devil who, sensing that Faust's soul is ripe for the plucking, begins to follow him in the guise of a black poodle. Faust is suspicious of the dog from the beginning, especially when it follows him into his study. But when the poodle begins to whine and howl as Faust is reading the Prologue to the Gospel of St. John—pondering how to translate the word "Logos"—he begins to suspect that he is a devil in disguise. By means of a special incantation the learned professor forces Mephistopheles to shed his canine form and appear in his human form.

Then begins a series of dialogue between Faust and Mephistopheles, in which the devilish Mephistopheles coaxes Faust to share with him more of his problem. In these illuminating verses Faust tells us again of his plight:

No matter what might be my own attire,
I would feel life cramped anyway.
I am too old merely to play,
Too young to be without desire.
What can the world give me? Renounce,
Renounce shalt thou, thou shalt renounce!
That is the everlasting song
Dinned in our ears throughout the course
Of all our lives, which all life long
Each hour sings until it's hoarse.
Mornings I wake with horror and could weep
Hot tears at seeing the new sun
Which will not grant me in its sweep

Fulfillment of a single wish, not one,
Which mars anticipated joys
Themselves with wilful captiousness
And with a thousand petty frets destroys
My eager heart's creativeness.
At nightfall I must lie down ill at ease
Upon my couch of misery where
There will be neither rest nor peace,
Wild dreams will terrify me even there.
The god that in my heart abides
Can stir my soul's profoundest springs;
He over all my energies presides
But cannot alter outward things.
Existence is a weight by which I am oppressed,
With death desired, life something to detest.
                                      (Lines 1544–1571)

Small wonder that Mephistopheles later calls Faust that "stick-in-the-mud Professor" (Line 3276).

The conversations between Faust and Mephistopheles culminate in an agreement between the two. Mephistopheles agrees to be Faust's servant in this life, and Faust, in return, agrees to give up his soul to the devil upon his death. Says Mephistopheles:

I'll bind myself to be your servant *here*
And at your beck and call wait tirelessly,
If when there in the *yonder* we appear
You will perform the same for me.   (Lines 1656–1659)

... Dare venture it. Just make
The compact, and I then will undertake
To turn my skills to joy. I'll give you more
Than any man has ever seen before.   (Lines 1671–1674)

Faust dares, and the agreement is reached, sealed in blood. For what does Faust ask? For a life of emotion, of color, of action. Not happiness as such, but a plunge into the maelstrom of life's boiling caldron is Faust's request:

> If ever I lie down upon a bed of ease,
> Then let that be my final end!
> If you can cozen me with lies
> Into a self-complacency,
> Or can beguile with pleasure you devise,
> Let that day be the last for me!   (Lines 1692–1697)

What Faust yearns for is revealing. He will exchange a life of contemplation for one of action, a life of ease for one of stress, a life of complacency for one of yearning. Perhaps most of all, he gives up his intellect for feeling; indeed, he even declares, "Feeling is everything" (Line 3456).

This tells us the way Faust is trying to renew himself, as well as the nature of the devilish Mephistopheles. Faust is abandoning his old Ego orientation, giving up his superior function of thinking, and is plunging into his un-lived life with the inferior function of feeling. He is like a man who can no longer stand to be safely on an intellec-tual shore that has become for him a dry desert, and who plunges into the wildly raging sea of his emotions.

Mephistopheles personifies the unlived life within Faust. This is why he is so devilish, for the unlived life is chaotic, and, having been the object of repression for so many years, tends to come back with a devilish capacity to overwhelm, beguile, and create chaos where before there was order. And yet it is not evil, nor is Mephistoph-eles evil, but, rather, the agent of change. This is why, when Mephistopheles was asked who he was, he replied,

Part of that Force which would
Do evil ever yet forever works the good.

(Lines 1336–1337)

For if order is good insofar as it safeguards against chaos, it is also evil because it tends to prevent the development of new forms of life. And if chaos is evil because it can destroy order, it can also be good because it can bring new energy. We are up against the old problem that William Blake once stated as the task of uniting the form of heaven with the energy of hell.

The story of Faust tells us what gives the unconscious its doubtful reputation and its paradoxical nature. The unlived life within us, when it first comes up, can be chaotic, overwhelming, and destructive. Small wonder an anxious Ego tries to keep it down, even at the price of life's vitality. Yet those unconscious energies within us are the very energies that can renew us. Devilish though these powers may seem to be, the Exhausted Ego may have to bargain with them if life is to be continued.

Mephistopheles keeps his bargain. He takes Faust to a witch who brews a noxious brew that has the power to renew youth, which Faust drinks and becomes a young man of twenty. He is then led to his many extraverted adventures which, naturally enough, considering Faust's recklessness and inexperience in the area of love and action and emotion, lead to disaster.

Spurning the drunken orgies of taverns that Mephistopheles first offers to him, Faust demands that he be led to genuine living. He is then led to a vision of the beautiful young Gretchen, and promptly becomes caught in "Love's entangled chains and ties" (Line 6567). He demands that Mephistopheles make it possible for him to have the girl, a ruse is concocted, and Gretchen falls in love with Faust, whose chivalrous feelings toward her are eclipsed by his passion. The result of their union is a child, a sword duel between Faust and Gretchen's brother, Valentine, which ends in the death of the latter, and ultimately brings about first the imprisonment and then the death of Faust's beloved Gretchen. The fact that Gretchen is taken tenderly to heaven is no comfort to Faust whose heart is ravaged by guilt and unfulfilled love. His plunge into life's boiling cauldron has been painful, but it has brought him the cup of life from which he has drunk. He now suffers, but is alive, no longer stranded on the empty desert of his soul.

So ends the first part of Goethe's drama. The second part was finished about half a century after the first and is entirely different. The first part shows Faust seeking what we might call an extraverted solution to his dilemma. If originally Faust was an introverted person thinking his way through life, contemplating life but never living it, now he has lived as an extravert who has plunged himself emotionally into life to live it without benefit of reflection upon it. In Part II Goethe resorts to imagination to solve Professor Faust's dilemma. To study this part of Goethe's play would take us far beyond the bounds of this book, but suffice it to say that it seems to represent an attempt to tap into the unlived life that is in the unconscious by means of imagination. We could say that it represents an introverted rather than an extraverted solution.

When Faust is finally a very old man he goes at last to his death full of experiences, sins, guilt, and glorious deeds. The devil hovers anxiously over his corpse waiting for his soul to emerge so that he can take it to hell. Certainly the devil has earned his prize, for he has kept his bargain and faithfully served Faust as his servant, bringing him the experiences he desired. Yet now at the very end he will be cheated, not by Faust, who is quite helpless to save himself, but by God, who decides to intervene and free Faust from the bargain he made. So at the moment Faust's soul appears, Mephistopheles' attention is momentarily distracted by cherubs sent from heaven, and at that instant the angels swoop down and carry Faust's soul safely away.

It may shock the morally conventional that God reckoned Faust's life fit for salvation after he had wreaked so much havoc in the lives of others, and lived with Mephistopheles as his dubious companion. But perhaps Goethe saw God in the same light as Jesus saw Him, when He proclaimed in the story of Luke 7:36–50, which we have already examined, that the woman who was a sinner was closer to salvation than the pious, safety-seeking Simon the Pharisee. It is at least in the spirit of Goethe himself that God would save Faust at the end, for Goethe saw the meaning of life as a process of soul-making in which there was to be forged a "distinct and durable personality" that could survive death (p. lxxxi).

As we have seen, in Part I Goethe showed us how Faust first tried to solve the dilemma of the Exhausted Ego by plunging into the opposite side of life, but in Part II a different way is followed. It is fitting that it be this way, for there are no rules for solving this problem. As we have seen, no one who is faced with the Faustian problem of the Exhausted Ego can find a collective answer. The one thing we can know for sure is that if a person contacts the unlived life within he will find new energy *and* new problems. Uniting the form of heaven and the energy of hell is not easy; it is bound to be a perilous undertaking, one which will challenge us to the utmost. The Exhausted Ego finds new life not through

repose and rest, but through a life of a different and renewed activity, whether this be expressed inwardly or
outwardly. It is not rest that restores, except temporarily,
but tapping into the energies within us that we have not
yet used.

This is seen even more clearly in the second tale we
will consider, the great medieval Legend of the Holy
Grail.

For centuries the Legend of the Holy Grail fascinat-
ed the Christian world, and in our time the story has
been brought alive for us again by the writings of Emma
Jung and Robert Johnson. It is Johnson to whom we are
primarily indebted for the insights that are presented
here, and many readers will want to read his book *HE!* in
order to study in depth what he has to say.

According to legend, Joseph of Arimathea used a
chalice to catch the blood of Christ as he was dying on
the Cross. Later Joseph took the chalice to England
where it was hidden in a castle. The chalice became
known as the Holy Grail and the castle as the Grail Castle, and it was said that whoever found the chalice and
correctly answered the question "Whom does the Grail
serve?" would be able to drink of it and find healing and
renewal for himself and for others. But none could find
it, for the Grail Castle could only be discovered by a
knight whose heart was pure, and though many searched
for it, the Grail Castle always eluded them.

The Grail Castle was ruled over by the Grail King,
who was known as the Wounded Fisher King because he
had years before accidentally wounded himself on a fish
by burning his hand in the fire in which the fish was
cooking when he reached in for a morsel. The wound
from the fish refused to heal, and extended to the King's
thigh where it affected his sexual potency. So the King

became ill and could not be cured, yet neither could he die.

Strangely enough, although the Holy Grail alone could cure the King, and although the Fisher King was King of the Grail Castle, he was not able to partake of the Grail himself. For the King to be cured, someone else had to find the Grail Castle and administer the chalice to him.

The King's wound was grievous. Because of it he had to be carried everywhere, his strength was gone, and his virility had all but perished. The sickness of the King extended to the whole land, which suffered a malaise as terrible as that of the King; nothing would grow, the animals would not reproduce, and the people went about in despair. As Robert Johnson tells us:

> The Grail Castle is in trouble. The Fisher King, the king of the castle, has been wounded. His wounds are so severe that he cannot live, yet he is incapable of dying. He groans, he cries out, he suffers all of the time. In fact, the whole land is in desolation. The cattle do not reproduce, the crops won't grow, knights are killed, children are orphaned, maidens weep, there is mourning everywhere—all because the Fisher King is wounded.

The picture that the legend paints of the wounded Fisher King is a vivid portrayal of the Exhausted Ego. It represents a ruling dominant of the conscious personality that has become so ill its life force is gone. As a result, all of life is impaired. The failure of crops to grow or animals to mate represents the lack of creativity in the life of a person with an Exhausted Ego. The general malaise of the land and the unhappiness of the people resembles the pervading depression that comes over us when we are exhausted, and the incurable condition of the Fisher King shows us that the Exhausted Ego faces a hopeless situation—unless help is received from another source. Just as the Fisher King cannot help himself, so the Exhausted Ego cannot, on its own strength, find a cure.

In the Legend of the Holy Grail help comes from an unusual source. The potential hero who might be able to cure the King and relieve the land is a strange, humble and uncouth youth who lives alone with his mother in the forest. His mother took him there because his father and all of his brothers had been killed serving as knights and she does not want to lose her remaining son. So the boy grows up in his isolated, forested world, and might have remained there forever except that one day he saw five magnificent men riding through the forest on richly apparalled horses. Dazzled by their glory he inquires about them and finds out that they are knights. Then, in spite of his mother's protests, the young man is determined that he too must become a knight. With this begins the many adventures that make up the bulk of the Legend of the Holy Grail.

The name of the young man is Parsifal, which means, "the Young Fool." It is a strange name for a hero, yet apt, for, as Johnson points out, Parsifal represents the unused, unsophisticated energies within us of which we are not aware. Of course we feel, and sometimes are, foolish when we experience these untapped resources in ourselves. A learned professor may feel awkward in a love affair, a gifted poet may look ridiculous trying to fix the plumbing, a man skilled with words may feel child-like trying to paint a picture. So whenever we depart from the area of our developed function and allow our-

selves to experience our undeveloped side we experience our foolishness.

The saving power of foolishness is not unknown to
the Christian world, for St. Paul compared the Cross itself to folly. In 1 Corinthians (1:21–25) he says:

> Do you see now how God has shown up the foolish-
> ness of human wisdom? If it was God's wisdom that
> human wisdom should not know God, it was because
> God wanted to save those who have faith through the
> foolishness of the message that we preach. And so,
> while the Jews demand miracles and the Greeks look
> for wisdom, here we are preaching a crucified Christ;
> to the Jews an obstacle that they cannot get over, to
> the pagans madness, but to those who have been
> called, whether they are Jews or Greeks, a Christ
> who is the power and wisdom of God. For God's fool-
> ishness is wiser than human wisdom, and God's
> weakness is stronger than human strength.

It would take us beyond the confines of this book to
explore the many adventures of Parsifal and their meaning, and Robert Johnson has already done it admirably in
his book. But we can ask what is the meaning of the question that must be correctly answered by the person who
discovers the Grail Castle. ("Whom does the Grail
serve?") Johnson says that the correct answer is, "The
Grail King." The incorrect answer would be, "Myself."
In short, the cure is not possible unless the personality is
reorganized, and moves from the Ego as the Center, to
the Self as the Center. Just as the earth is not the center
of the solar system, neither is the Ego the center of the
personality. And just as the sun is the proper center of
the solar system, so at the center of the personality there

is a greater reality than the Ego, called by the early Christian world the Christ within.

So the Legend of the Holy Grail tells us what must be done if the Exhausted Ego is to be healed: a new energy must come up from the realms of the unconscious, even though it brings with it the taint of foolishness, and a new center to the personality must be acknoweldged that is greater than that of the Ego and its concerns. Achieving this represents a monumental spiritual journey, and the many tales in the Legend of the Holy Grail tell us more about the difficulties of this journey and how it is accomplished. For us at this time it is enough to note that the solution to the problem of our deeper exhaustion is to undertake what we would call in religious language a spiritual pilgrimage or search for God, and what the modern depth psychologist might call individuation, or the search for wholeness.

12

Finding Energy Again

In the introduction we noted that the word "burn-out" is related to the symbolism of fire, and that fire is a form of energy. Fire may burn brightly and creatively, it may rage out of control and be destructive, or it may die out by consuming itself. We also noted in the introduction that each of us has a certain amount of psychic energy (also called libido) and this psychic energy can be likened to fire. In our examination of the story of Faust and the Legend of the Holy Grail we saw that psychic energy can be consumed, and then new sources of energy must be found. It may help us to look more closely at how energy works, in the hope that we can find ways to renew energy when it becomes depleted.

The science of physics has a word for the running down of energy: entropy.[1] Entropy refers to the phenomenon in which energy in a consolidated form dissipates itself into a diffused form. When energy is in a diffused form it is not available to us. For instance, the energy in a log can be burned, but in the process of combustion the energy escapes from the log in the form of

---

[1] I am indebted to my friend, Steve Hartwell, for pointing out to me the significance for psychology of this idea of entropy.

heat and gases and is then no longer available for use. The idea in physics is that all energy is in a state of entropy. For instance, the sun is gradually dissipating its energy in atomic explosions. Clearly if energy is constantly undergoing entropy the world is running down, just as a human being who only dissipates energy will run down (we even speak of "being run down" when we are worn out with work, worry, or physical exertion).

Fortunately, nature also has examples of the reverse process: the consolidation of energy from more diffused to more consolidated forms. In plant life this is called photosynthesis, a process in which a plant forms carbohydrates from water and carbon dioxide, and builds up chlorophyll-containing tissues that are exposed to light. In this way cells are built up and plant life develops. In animal life, including human life, we have metabolism, a process in which the body builds up complex living protoplasm from various nutritive substances found in our food. We can think of psychic energy in somewhat the same way: it is always breaking down, and must always be built up again.

Another image is that of a lake. Being from California I like to picture a lake high up in the rugged Sierra Nevada, a blue jewel suspended just below the sky with marvelously clear, pure and sparkling water. For such a lake to exist two things are necessary: an outlet for its waters, and one or more inlets so water can come into it.

One is as necessary as the other. If a lake has no outlet the water will become stagnant and clogged with all kinds of foreign materials; it will be a kind of sink-hole rather than a lake. Fortunately, the lakes in the Sierra Nevada have outlets from which the clear waters pour out over the rocks and tumble down the mountainside, creating deep pools for the fish and lush places for unusual vegetation to grow. This stream of water flowing out of the lake is essential for the vitality of the lake which, filled to overflowing, spills over into its outgoing stream.

In the life of a human being, the equivalent of the outgoing stream is the flow of energy that pours out of a person and into life. Most of this outflow of energy goes into work, play, or relationships. For this reason, if the flow of energy is to take place a person needs worthwhile work, creative play, and meaningful relationships. If these ingredients are not there, the stream of psychic energy will not flow, and the result will be a deadening of our energies. For that is the mystery of our energy: like the water in a lake, it cannot stand still; it must flow in order to be healthy. A human being can only conserve energy for a limited time before it turns negative. Like a runner who rests several days before a strenuous race, we store up energy for some purpose, but only for a short while. In the long run, if we do not have an appropriate outlet for our energy we lose it, and then we feel listless or empty. We are like a lake whose waters have become dead.

For this reason any block to our flow of energy is a threat to our well-being. If a person's work is boring, that is a threat to his life vitality. If someone loses people she loves, that too is a threat to life, and may even lead to illness, as James Lynch has shown in his masterful book, *The Broken Heart.*

A person must also have a source of energy, just as a lake must have a source of energy. A human being cannot always pour energy out; there must also be times when energy comes back in. Ebb tide must be followed by high tide, nutrients taken from the soil as we grow our food must be replaced, and the energy that goes out of us must also be replenished.

Sometimes when we feel depleted of energy it may help to close our eyes, become relaxed, shut out the outer world for the time being, and picture a lake. The image that comes to our minds may show us where we are. Is the lake full and brimming? Is the lake stagnant and blocked up? Is the lake becoming drained and empty? So it may be with our energy. If we then picture streams flowing into the lake, renewing it, we may help energy recreate itself within us.

Fortunately for us, life provides us with many sources of energy. In the Grail Legend the Grail can never be exhausted; it symbolizes life's power to continually renew itself. In Greek mythology there is also such an image: Antaeus, whose strength was always renewed as long as he was in touch with the earth. And in the New Testament, as we have already noted, there is an emphasis upon the symbolism of food, culminating in the rite of the Eucharist, in which the body and blood of Christ become a food for us that can never be exhausted. So the sources of new energy are there, if only we can find them.

It would go beyond the boundaries of this book to go deeply into the matter of finding sources for new energy; also I have already touched on some of this in the last chapter of my book *Healing and Wholeness*. However, it is fitting to mention some of the places where we can look for new sources of energy, as long as we remember that each person is an individual, and what may be a source of energy for one person may not be a source of energy for someone else.

1. *A change of outer activity.* We have mentioned in previous chapters that a change of outer activity may be helpful in curing Burnout. Such a change can help us

draw on new sources of energy that were always there, but were not flowing because they had no way to come into our lives. Generally, as we have seen, the helpful outer activity will be something entirely different than our regular line of work.

2. *Creative relationships.* We have mentioned this also and I include it here only so that our list will be more or less complete. Relationships require energy, but also give us energy. A true relationship is an effort; we must put energy into it in order to get energy from it. But relationships that are based on personal factors (not professional ones) are creative sources of energy because they keep energy moving and flowing, and provide a vital outlet for our Eros, without which life quickly loses its meaning.

3. *Using the body creatively.* When most ministering persons say they are exhausted, they mean that they are spiritually exhausted. Of course the feeling of exhaustion may also extend to the body. Physically we may feel languid and lacking in vitality, because the spirit quickens the body just as the body is the physical basis for the life of the spirit.

This is worth a further comment. In our culture we are used to thinking of the body as the basis for the life of the personality. When someone dies, the personality also dies (so we think). It is true that our personality, our spiritual life force, cannot be strong if our body is ill or weak, and this is why it is so important that we try to maintain the health of the body (through proper nutrition, among other things). The Bible was wise in referring to the body as the temple of the Spirit, for the two are joined together, at least in this life.

But the opposite is also true: the spirit quickens the body. In fact, this is the older of the two ideas. We are told in the Book of Genesis that when God created Adam he made a man out of clay and then breathed into the clay the breath of life; so an infusion of spirit made the clay alive and brought Adam into existence. Ancient people believed that the body lived because it had a spirit within it; when a person breathed his last breath, that was the spirit departing from the body, and so the body was now inert and lifeless. It was the opposite from our modern idea that personality is derived from the body, but both ideas can be said to be true, for, as psychosomatic medicine has shown, when the spirit is weak the body may become ill, just as when the body is weak the spirit may suffer.

So when those of us who work with our minds, our spirits, and our emotions feel exhausted and physically depleted, we need to remember that while our bodies are feeling the effect of our disorder, the body itself is not depleted. In fact, the cells of the body may be stored with glycogen, physically ready for action because our work has not required its use. Thus the body may be the source for new energy; use of the body may get energy moving again and revive us spiritually.

The two most important things about our choice of physical movement are that the physical activity is interesting to us and that it requires deep breathing. If we are bored with our physical activity, we probably will not do it. If we find it interesting, we will amost certainly pursue it. Veteran joggers report that they never get bored while running (there is always too much to think about), but other people report that they cannot stand running because it is so monotonous. So we need to choose the kind of physical activity that most interests us. But it is important that it be strenuous enough to produce deep breathing. Shallow breathing has been connected with states of depression and anxiety, and also with adverse lung conditions. Deep breathing reverses the tendency to despondency, and so has a healing and rejuvenating effect on us spiritually as well as physically. For persons in the ministry this is especially important, since our work is, for the most part, sedentary, and our breathing can become quite shallow without our realizing it.

As we have said, physical movement gets energy moving again and will help us when we are spiritually depleted. It also helps just because we are in better condition. Work that is mental and spiritual requires good physical conditioning just as much as strenuous physical work does.

There is an interesting example of this: the Swiss chess grandmaster, Victor Korchnoi, is old for a champion chess player. He was forty-seven when he first played Anatoly Karpov for the world championship. Karpov, being only twenty-seven, had an advantage because chess is a game of concentration, and as we age our powers of concentration wane along with many other things. So Korchnoi engaged in a regimen of jogging and yoga in order to be in condition to play chess. In the match that ensued he came within a whisker of defeating his younger adversary, and at this writing has won the right to challenge Karpov for the championship once again.

4. *Meditation.* Now we can turn to the more inward ways of contacting energy, and meditation is one of the most important. I have already mentioned that it sometimes helps when we need energy to meditate on a lake. Meditation helps us find energy because it puts us in touch with the living images that come up from the soul,

and these images have a power and autonomous life all their own. To find them and contemplate images from the unconscious is to draw energy up into oneself, and thus renew one's conscious life. In this book I am not going to say more about meditation because it is such a rich and complex subject, but in addition to the comments on it in *Healing and Wholeness,* which I have already mentioned, I refer the reader to Morton T. Kelsey's excellent book on the subject, *The Other Side of Silence.*

5. *Dreams.* Here is another rich source of energy. To record a dream, contemplate it, and relate to it through meditation, painting it, or discussing it with a friend or counselor, is to come into contact with a certain quantity of energy. The unconscious is full of energy; it is only the Ego that becomes depleted. A dream has energy in it, and proper use of the dream transfers energy from the unconscious into consciousness where it is available for use. Recording and studying our dreams is a little like being able to go to the bank and draw out money when we need it.

There is good reason for a Christian to make the study of dreams part of one's devotional life, for the Bible and the early Church are full of dreams and repeatedly stress their importance in spiritual life. I am not going to say more on dreams here because I have already written two books on the subject, *Dreams: God's Forgotten Language,* and *Dreams and Healing.* There are many other helpful books on dreams too, including Morton T. Kelsey's succinct volume, *Dreams: A Way to Listen to God.*

6. *Keeping a Journal.* A Journal is a book in which we record all matters of importance for our conscious

life. We write down our dreams, our fantasies, our urges, and our creative thoughts. In our Journal we write out our problems, what is worrying us, what is getting us down, and our darkest, most unthinkable thoughts. Anything of importance to the life of the soul can be written in our Journal.

This is helpful because it gives us a perspective on our personal difficulties so that we will not be overcome by them, and because it keeps the creative thoughts and helpful images from disappearing. Writing down creative ideas is like planting seeds in a garden—once written down they can sprout and grow. Otherwise we are likely to lose the creative potential that lies in our dreams and sudden inspirations.

Keeping a Journal is a natural part of the Christian devotional life because it is cultivating a relationship with our soul, and, through the soul, with God. It is the most inexpensive form of psychotherapy I know; for about one dollar we can buy the notebook and pencil we need.

The Journal can be likened to a container. Without a container to hold it, water would spill out over the floor. Similarly, without some way to contain it, the vital life of the psyche spills and gets away from us. The Journal helps us contain the life of the psyche. Then we are like people with a swimming pool in the back yard; they can dive into the pool and swim whenever they need to because the pool contains the water. So with the Journal— we can dive into the life of our soul and it will be there for us and will not be lost.

It is simple to keep a Journal—just start writing things down. But there are also aids to Journal keeping. Ira Progoff has done much good work here with books

and conferences, and Morton Kelsey has helpful suggestions in his book, *Adventure Inward: Christian Growth
Through Personal Journal Writing.*

7. *Paying attention to our fantasies.* Fantasies are
those autonomous trains of thought that find their way
into our consciousness without our inviting them in.
They may vary from chance thoughts or random impulses to coherent fantasy stories. When we deliberately
cultivate a fantasy because it brings us pleasure we speak
of it as a daydream, but most fantasies just come and
present themselves to us as they are.

Fantasies are part of the undirected thinking of the
mind, in contrast to the directed thinking of the Ego.
The Ego directs its thoughts. We say, "Now I am going to
work on this problem," and we think about it. Fantasies
are not directed by the Ego, but by something else in us
of which we are unconscious.

When we have a fantasy we need to remember that
there is a certain amount of energy behind it. It is this
energy that keeps the fantasy going. It may be only a
small amount of energy, or it may be a great deal, in
which case the fantasy will come back again and again.
(A sexual fantasy would be an example.)

Most people disregard their fantasies. They try to get
rid of them by ignoring them or shoving them aside; they
treat them like waste material to be flushed down the
toilet. We do this partly because we are trained to believe that fantasy material is worthless, and so we pay no
attention. However, sometimes we try to rid ourselves of
our fantasies because we are shocked by them. We may
have been taught to regard certain fantasies as evil, and
to be afraid of "dark" fantasies, such as those centering

around certain sexual desires, ill-will toward other people, or impending disasters. We need to remember that only *actions* are evil, not fantasies. Everyone has dark fantasies. Merely having a fantasy is not in itself a sin, although it might be a sin if we acted it out. For instance, if we are angry at someone and have a fantasy that she is dead, we have not sinned. Only if we actually injure that person have we perhaps committed a sin.

This is important because we need to be at home with our own thoughts, and if they frighten us, it is as though we are afraid of ourselves. If dark fantasies that we cannot come to terms with persist, perhaps we need to share them with a spiritual director or therapist and work them through. But they should not be disregarded, for fantasies call attention to a certain kind of energy in the soul, and often offer us helpful guidance as well.

A helpful fantasy is one that contains hints about what we might do to renew our life. It is the energy in fantasies that enables them to reach consciousness. If we lack something on the level of our conscious life, we may fantasize about exactly what we need to do to fill this emptiness.

For instance, if we are terribly thirsty we will have fantasies about something to drink. We will find ourselves thinking, "When I get home from this hot hike I am going to make myself a tall glass of iced tea—or maybe orange juice would taste better—or lemonade." We are dehydrated, and the fantasy is the body's way of telling us what we need. The spirit, too, can tell us what we need by means of a fantasy. We may find that we are imagining ourselves hiking in the mountains, fishing by a cool mountain stream, swimming in a lake, or reading a book quietly in the library, and something like this may

be exactly what we need to do in order to renew ourselves. In such ways we are given clues about where new
life may be found.

In *Healing and Wholeness* I tell the story of a man
who was terribly depressed but had to perform at a con-
cert that evening. He talked his depression over with me
but nothing seemed to help. However, on leaving my office he had the fantasy of going to the ocean, so he went
and waded into the water fully clothed and stood in the
waves for forty-five minutes. When he emerged his depression was gone, and he had the energy he needed for
his musical performance.

8. *Active Imagination.* Active Imagination is a spiritual and psychological technique that is like meditation
but goes beyond it because the Ego is more active in the
process. Out of the unconscious come spontaneous images and thoughts. We do not ask for these images and
thoughts; they just come to us—in dreams, fantasies, or
waking trains of thought. In meditation we may select
one of these images and focus on it in order to integrate
that image into our souls. In Active Imagination we not
only focus on the images, or recall the thoughts we are
having, but we interact with them deliberately. In this
way the Ego and the unconscious can "have it out," or
can approach more closely to each other.

We have already seen two examples of Active Imagination in this book. The first came in Chapter 5 where it
was suggested that we might carry on a dialogue with the
Inner Monitor. The second example is in the story of Elijah, for Elijah's talk with God in the cave on Mount Sinai
is a good example of Active Imagination. However, I am
not going to describe this process in any more detail here
because I have already done so in two of my books, *Healing and Wholeness* and *Dreams and Healing,* and others,

such as Morton Kelsey and C. G. Jung (who originated the term Active Imagination and first developed it as a psychological technique) have also done so. I have included Active Imagination here in order that the list of aids to renewing energy may be *more* complete. Note that this is *not* a *complete* list.

Life is varied, complex, individual, and ceaselessly creative, and it would be impossible to describe all the ways that psychic life can renew itself. Nor is it possible in any book to offer a particular reader *his* way of working with himself to renew his life. No two cooks ever cook the same even if they follow the same recipe, and in the matter of energy renewal, each person is his own cook.

This book, and especially this last chapter, can be looked upon as a kind of cookbook: a list of recipes that have proved useful to some people. Such books are often helpful, but they are no substitute for the imagination, creativity, and resourcefulness that God can send to each person who struggles with his or her problem of Burnout in order to find a new direction for life.

Bibliography

Guggenbuhl-Craig, Adolf. *Eros on Crutches*. Irving, Texas: Spring Publications, 1980.

——*Power in the Helping Professions*. New York: Spring Publications, 1971.

Johnson, Robert. *HE!* King of Prussia, Pa.: Religious Publishing Co., 1974.

Kelsey, Morton T. *Adventure Inward: Christian Growth Through Personal Journal Writing*. Minneapolis, Minn.: Augsburg Publishing House, 1980.

——*Dreams: A Way to Listen to God*. New York: Paulist Press, 1978.

——*The Other Side of Silence*. New York: Paulist Press, 1976.

Kunkel, Fritz. *How Character Develops*. Out of print.

——*In Search of Maturity*. Out of print.

——*Creation Continues*. New York: Charles Scribner's Sons, 1952. Reprinted by Word Books, Inc., Waco, Texas, 1973.

Lynch, James. *The Broken Heart: The Medical Consequences of Loneliness*. New York: Basic Books, Inc., 1979.

Sanford, John A. *Between People*. New York: Paulist Press, 1982.

————*Dreams: God's Forgotten Language.* New York: Lippincott Publishing Co., 1968.

————*Dreams and Healing.* New York: Paulist Press, 1978.

————*Evil: The Shadow Side of Reality.* New York: Crossroad, 1981.

————*Healing and Wholeness.* New York: Paulist Press, 1977.

————*The Kingdom Within.* New York: J. B. Lippincott Co., 1970; New York: Paulist Press, 1980.

————*The Invisible Partners.* New York. Paulist Press, 1980.

von Franz, Marie-Louise. *The Feminine in Fairy Tales.* Zurich: Spring Publications, 1972.

von Goethe, Johann Wolfgang. *Faust.* tr. Charles E. Passage. Library of Liberal Arts, Bobbs-Merrill, Inc., 1965.